SMALL BRAND AMERICA II

A look at 25 more tiny U.S. brands succeeding in a world dominated by giant competitors

BY
STEVE AKLEY

To Rose Sarkisian, "The First Lady of Specialty Coffee":

Your personal and professional stories encapsulate exactly what *Small Brand America* is all about – intriguing, inventive, industrious, interesting and inspirational.

Keep brewing, my friend!

Preface

The success of my first book in the series, **Small Brand America**, was nothing short of amazing. The stories of small brands competing against large multinational "megabrands" seemed to hit home with not only readers but other small brands. The work in finding 25 companies to highlight in the follow-up was clearly much easier the second time around with both readers recommending other companies to feature and even companies reaching out to me to request to be in the sequel.

The approach here is the same successful formula which was established in the first book. We have 25 companies featured, each with a 10-page profile which includes basic contact information, an in-depth biography of both the company and the owners, and a photo album.

Just like the first time around, you will find 25 companies, each with an individual story of intrigue and triumph. We are talking individuals who were willing to take on companies which have resources that afford them the luxury of being able to outspend and outman these tiny companies.

I have noticed, over the course of meeting the 50+ individuals I have interviewed for these two books, that just because the megabrands have superior resources available to them doesn't mean they have a better product. In fact, I have found it to be quite the opposite. The companies with the greater resources, and the products which are often household names, are nowhere near the quality of the small companies.

The economies of scale actually tilt an advantage towards the small companies. The small batch approach utilized by small companies means saving a few pennies by cutting a corner here and there has very minimal impact on the bottom line. Since there is so little net impact on the profits of the small brands, they tend to not take these short cuts.

For the megabrands the story is very different. Saving even a fraction of a penny can mean substantial savings when discussing production runs of thousand, hundreds of thousands or even millions. Every ounce of profit cut out has a huge effect on the profitability of the large companies. This means the quality of products is often sacrificed for the sake of profitability. The investment of a lower quality product is then protected with payments to grocers for shelf space and large advertising budgets. This works great for the system, but not necessarily for the consumer.

Telling the stories of companies doing things right is fun for me as an author, and I believe you will find their stories enjoyable as a reader. The ultimate compliment for me would to not only provide you an enjoyable reading experience but to introduce you to some new products you can enjoy as well.

After all, each one represents **Small Brand America**!

Table of Contents

Chapter 1: Bacon
Denver Bacon Company

P.O. Box 6
Denver, CO 80201

denverbacon.com
denverbaconcompany@gmail.com

Established
2013

Leadership
Eric Clayman and Chef Justin Brunson, Co-Founders

Products
Artisan bacon with more products coming to the market soon

Seems like they will transition from *Small Brand America* to *Large Brand America* in about 15 minutes…

In "19 aught 3" "Grandpappy" Ezekiel Clayman partnered with Chef Jebidiah Brunson to chip in and buy Box #6 at the Denver Post Office and form the Denver Bacon Company.

Truth be told, the company wasn't actually formed until 2013 when Eric Clayman partnered with Chef Justin Brunson. No one actually knows how they managed to secure P.O. Box #6 in Denver's original zip code.

It does appear Eric and Justin have packed a lot of history in the year they have been in business. They seem to be like watching a movie in fast forward, and it very well might be if your movie ends up with two guys taking the bacon world by storm.

Eric grew up in Orlando. He went to college at Tulane in New Orleans where he got his first exposure to the culinary world with all of the great restaurants in the area. After college, he had a friend who had access to a condo in Vail and a job offer at a ski shop.

Who wouldn't jump at that?

After five years of various jobs in marketing for resorts and lodges in Vail, he moved with a girlfriend to New York City. When the relationship ended, he moved back to Colorado and started a business development sales and consulting firm, specializing in the grocery industry.

One day he was working on selling one of the lines he represented, and he called on a bakery to see if they were interested in his cookie line. While they weren't interested in the cookies (they were a bakery after all), the owner did like his presentation. He thought Eric's company might be able to assist him in getting a shelf stable granola they had been baking to market. He was a baker; he didn't have the experience needed to launch a brand.

Ultimately, Eric was brought in as a partner to help get the granola product going. Within three years, they went from a hobby for a baker to a nationally distributed product. Despite the success, competition was tough, and the battle wasn't over. They were going to need to continue to innovate and hustle to keep growing the company.

One day, one of their bakers requested they try a new gluten-free product line he had been working on. The management team agreed it was good, but not as good as their regular line. When the baker encouraged them to read up on gluten and the growing contingent of consumers turning away from gluten-based products, they agreed to do so. After learning more, they decided to give the line a try through the channels they had already built with their granola.

Within 18 months, they were the top selling gluten-free line in the country. Facing a multi-million dollar equipment investment to scale-up to continue to grow the brand, they were ripe for a buyout, which is exactly what they ended up doing.

Eric Clayman had made the wild ride of launching a brand to gaining national distribution to being bought out by a megabrand. Now he was out of work. Lucky for him, Chef Justin Brunson was looking for someone to help him launch a brand he had been toying with as well.

Justin Brunson grew up in Iowa. His youth was spent hunting, fishing and gardening. It was during his upbringing in Iowa that he would gain the foundation he would use in his culinary skills decades later.

After receiving his formal training in Arizona at the prestigious LeCordon Bleu College of Culinary Arts, he held a variety of progressively higher profile chef positions, all culminating in

2008 when he opened up his own restaurant, the Masterpiece Deli (*masterpiecedeli.com*).

Unlike your typical sandwich shop, featuring sliced meats from well-known national brands, Justin took the artisanal approach of doing everything himself at Masterpiece Deli. From the meats to the condiments to the sides, he stood out by bringing a fine dining approach to his sandwiches.

One of his most popular menu items was his bacon. Like everything at Masterpiece Deli, he did it all: buying pork bellies, seasoning it, smoking it and slicing it. Customers always inquired about buying some so they could prepare it at home.

A mutual friend, who familiar with the fact Justin was looking to launch a brand, and knowing Eric had experience in doing that with the granola company, introduced the two. A partnership was formed, and they set out to launch a bacon company.

As a marketing expert, Eric was ready to expand on the idea of the Masterpiece Deli and brand the bacon under the name of the restaurant. With his knowledge of the restaurant business, Justin was a little reluctant to go that route. He foresaw the local restaurant market as a solid avenue to sell their bacon. He thought chefs might be hesitant to offer bacon branded with the name of another restaurant on it.

They toyed with the ideas of incorporating Rocky Mountain or Mile High in the name, but they seemed played out to them. When they came up with the Denver Bacon Company, they had a name that told who they were and also connected people with its flowing "DBC" nickname.

Going from a house-made bacon at a restaurant to a consumer packaged product is a big leap. Not only is there a whole new level of inspections (local health inspectors for a restaurant versus the U.S. Department of Agriculture for a meat-based consumer packaged product), you have to find an approved packer, willing to do production runs suitable for a start-up.

The inspections, while cumbersome, were nowhere near as difficult as the obstacle of the small production runs they were seeking. The good news for them was the fact the Masterpiece Deli accounts for about 150 lbs. of bacon a week so they had their first customer secured right out of the gate: themselves!

They finally found a company willing to work with them, but the situation wasn't ideal. They specialized in pre-made meals for nationwide retailers so their expertise clearly wasn't bacon. That wasn't a great start, but the really troublesome issue was their plant used to produce bacon was for sale. If it was sold, they would be right back where they started.

With no other options, they went ahead with the partnership. They were officially in the bacon business, and they immediately started making inroads in the local market. Just two months later, the plant was bought out… not even by another meat company, but instead by an artist who was going to use the space for a studio.

Once again, DBC was looking for a packer. Lucky for them, their quick initial success had garnered some interest in the market. A second generation owner of a 40+ year old local packing company contacted them about taking over the production for them. They worked with him to get the recipe right, and in the fall of 2013 the new company not only began packing their bacon, they added it to their sales lineup. Their previous packer had been a pre-made meal expert, but the new company carried a variety of sausages and had wholesale customers like restaurants and stadiums which were a perfect fit for DBC's bacon.

In addition to the packing of the product, they also took over the production. This doesn't sound like much until you realize Eric and Justin spent a lot of their time coordinating the purchase of pork bellies to coincide with when their product could be processed and packed. Their timing had to be impeccable to fall exactly in conjunction with inventory needs. Now their new packer was handling all of that for them, freeing up Justin to focus on product development and his growing restaurant business (he opened a second restaurant, this one a fine dining establishment called Old Major/*oldmajordenver.com*) and Eric to work on marketing and growth of the Denver Bacon Company.

There seems to be plenty of growth ahead for DBC. They are working on several new product extensions. They should soon be introducing a maple bacon breakfast roll which is similar in look to the sliceable sausage rolls for sale in grocery stores today. The difference being their product is going to combine the tastes of bacon and sausage and should be the perfect choice for those who struggle with the question, "Bacon or sausage?"

They are not stopping there.

They also have perfected a process allowing them to incorporate bacon into confections. They have a lineup planned which includes products like bacon salted caramels, bacon toffee and bacon peanut brittle.

But wait, there's more.

Can you say bacon butter? It's true. The ultimate marriage to go with bacon's meaty and salty goodness: a butter and bacon combo.

These are not novelty items. These are seriously good products drawing upon the culinary expertise of Chef Justin Brunson and the marketing/distribution experience of Eric Clayman.

That may be as much as two people can pack into a one year old company.

Hmmm... P.O. Box #6.

Are we really sure this company isn't actually 111 years old?

Denver Bacon Company Photo Album

Eric Clayman and Chef Justin Brunson

Soon to be bacon (in the smoker)

Raw

Cooked

Chef Justin appearing on a local news segment

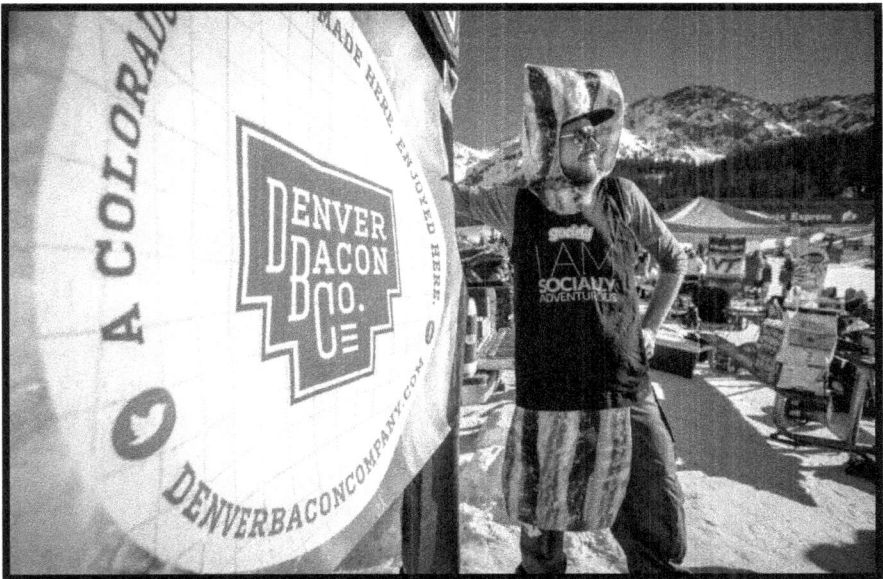

This is happening: a dude in a bacon suit

How bad do you want a sandwich from Justin now?

DENVER BACON CO.

DENVERBACON.COM

MADE OF THE FINEST SMOKE AND SWINE.

U.S. INSPECTED AND PASSED BY DEPARTMENT OF AGRICULTURE EST. 6432

A COLORADO CREATION —— MADE HERE —— ENJOYED EVERYWHERE

BUTCHER-CUT MAPLE BACON

DRY CURED + HARDWOOD SMOKED | KEEP REFRIGERATED | NET WT. 16 OZ. (1LB)

Close-up of DBC's label

Denver Bacon Company product lineup

Chapter 2: Barbecue Sauce
The James Gang BBQ Company

P.O. Box 853
Newberg, OR 97132
(503) 538 - 2830

jamesgangbbq.com
jamesgangbbq@frontier.com

Established
1996

Leadership
Pam and Jesse James, Owners

Products
Barbecue sauce in multiple flavors and levels of heat, spices and chili mix

"When we bought the restaurant, we didn't buy the sauce; that's okay, I'll make one."…

History has been kind to the Wild West outlaw Jesse James in the 130+ years since his death, Despite his role as a career criminal (robbery and murder), the romanticized tales of his crimes, and time on the run, have made him a part of American lore. He is studied in classrooms and been part of numerous movies and TV shows.

Jesse James, co-owner of The James Gang BBQ Company with his wife Pam, is the real deal and not a marketing gimmick. This southern Californian Jesse James was born to a mother from Missouri (home of the original Jesse James). She already had a son named Frank. (The same name as outlaw Jesse James' older brother.) She was considering the name John if her child was a boy but a group of friends talked her into going with Jesse, something her son would relish through the years (after all, people remember you when your name is Jesse James).

When his parents had some problems with break-ins at their home, they decided to follow Jesse's sister to Oregon. Jesse convinced Pam to join the rest of his family in 1993 in Oregon where they would end up buying a barbecue restaurant.

The plan was for Pam to run the restaurant, and Jesse was going to work in the evenings and on weekends but would be working full-time during the week at a dental equipment company.

There was one small problem with the restaurant. Many of the recipes on the menu were included in the purchase but Jesse and Pam were surprised a barbecue sauce recipe was not.

Even though they had assumed the sauce was included in the deal, Jesse declared it to be not a problem. He would simply develop his own.

With his first offerings a little too spicy for the patrons of their restaurant, it took him about a week of refining his ingredients to get the recipe where he was happy.

Once he got it right, he apparently really got it right. He was flattered that people would like his sauce so much they began to request to take it home. It wasn't an uncommon sight to have customers leaving with a bag of barbecue and a Styrofoam™ cup of sauce.

Soon, Jesse took his sauce to the next level by bottling it himself in mason jars in the kitchen. He was now able to sell his jarred sauce to customers in his restaurant. These weren't professional looking (Jesse printed the labels himself), but offering what appeared to be a store-bought sauce wasn't his goal. He was just trying to fulfill the demand he had created by serving it in his restaurant.

Since they owned a restaurant, Pam and Jesse made it a habit to attend food shows to look for ideas for the restaurant. It was at one of these shows they came across a vendor offering a bottling machine. The purchase of one of these machines would allow Jesse and Pam to offer a more professionally designed sauce in bottles which could be sealed and sold in stores. They decided to take the plunge and give it a try.

Jesse celebrated his new bottler by creating a second sauce. With two products in their line now, Pam and Jesse decided to bottle them under the name The James Gang BBQ Company, and their first attempt to sell them outside of the restaurant was to bring them to a food show. They sold some sauce at that show… make that a lot of sauce at that show!

It was readily apparent Jesse and Pam now had a second business on their hands. The year was 1996, and Jesse and Pam decided to take the next step by officially separating their sauce from their barbecue business and forming a second company.

Jesse began to test the waters with his sauces by entering them in some of the respected national barbecue contests. He couldn't believe when the first entry for his original "Famous" sauce placed in the top 20 out of over 500 entries!

He continued to create new sauces and enter them in these contests, and the awards just kept piling up. He was thrilled as can be with each victory.

While Jesse and Pam are "people persons," they are not salespeople. They never have been into the concept of aggressively selling their product. Lucky for them, the product speaks for itself. Through the word-of-mouth which came from their restaurant, and later some of the publicity surrounding their wins at the barbecue competitions, the word about The James Gang's sauces motivated stores to call them about carrying it on their shelves.

It seemed each call to them about carrying their sauces resulted in not only a new customer, but a new friend. One call Jesse took, he initially thought was a joke. He got a message from a man with a heavy German accent asking about buying pallets of his sauces and shipping them to Germany. Assuming it was a prank, Jesse didn't even follow-up.

When the man called a second time, he got Jesse live. He said he had walked store-to-store in town asking if anyone knew who the Jesse James was on the bottle of sauce he had. He had run into one of his barbecue sauce competitors who not only knew Jesse but had his number. He gave it to the man who then had started calling Jesse.

It turns out this was no prank. The man was a grill manufacturer in Germany. He wanted to include some authentic barbecue sauce with the purchase of one of this grills, and he preferred The James Gangs' sauce over anything he could find in his native Germany. By the end of the call, Jesse had an order for four pallets of sauce, and this has continued every couple of months since the initial phone call.

By 2000, their sauce was selling so well, they decided to make some major changes in their lives. First of all, Jesse decided to leave his job and its 130 mile daily roundtrip. This was a welcome relief for him since he was worn out from the commute. Plus, it was dangerous. He had to leave so early in the morning, he found himself trying to navigate roads with some of the local wildlife (he just missed an elk and did end up hitting a deer).

The other big change in the lives of the James family came from the fact they decided to sell their restaurant. Unlike the person they bought their restaurant from, they were very upfront that the sauce didn't go with the restaurant. (The new owner had stated he would keep the 10 year old restaurant a barbecue joint, but soon changed it to a bistro and was out of business within six months).

Their Whiskey Grilling sauce is their most popular offering. It's also been one of their most decorated products, having achieved top 10 status four times in national contests. It also won an award for label design which added another element of accolades to the trophy case of the James Gang.

More than anything, The James Gang BBQ Company is a love story. Approaching 65, Jesse admits he's not driven to be a huge success with his company. It's more about something he and Pam can do together. They love to travel and spend time together, and the company allows them to do both.

Not everyone believed their union would last. When 21 year old Jesse proposed to 16 year old Pam, they had to get the permission of her parents to get married. When Jesse told his boss he was getting married, his boss got him two bottles of champagne as a gift: one to celebrate his marriage and one to save to celebrate his inevitable divorce.

Forty-three year later the couple is still going strong and thanks to The James Gang, they are still having fun. If you get a chance to pick up a bottle of one of their award winning sauces, you might be able to join the fun as well!

The James Gang BBQ Company Photo Album

Pam and Jesse James

Now that's a pit

Pam working an event

Jesse barbecuing

Some of the James Gang's barbecue awards

At a trade show

Product detail for their Sweat Southern Heat Whiskey Grilling Sauce

The James Gang's product lineup

Chapter 3: Beef Jerky
Fatman's Beef Jerky

1600 South Main
Roswell, NM 88203
(575) 752 - 2333

fatmansbeefjerky.com
realmeatfoods@qwestoffice.net

Established
2006

Leadership
Rick and Ellen Robey, Owners

Products
Beef Jerky

Embracing the "Fatman" moniker like no one since William Conrad...

Rick Robey grew up in Chino, California. He started his first cattle ranch in California in the early 1970s. He expanded his operation by scaling up to a larger ranch in Texas and repeated the process to grow larger, yet again, with a move to New Mexico. At the height of his involvement in cattle ranching, he had a working ranch of over 2,500 acres with 30,000 cattle and 65 employees.

Running a large operation also carries a significant amount of risk.

Over the course of seven years, Rick experienced two disasters that dealt him severe financial blows. The first came in 1997. New Mexico experienced what was referred to as a "100 year snow storm." This blizzard, with its snow blowing in sideways, caused the calves to huddle up in the corner of the pens which, sadly, led to them trampling one another to death. Rick lost 7,000 calves that day.

Seven years later he was really just getting back on track when a rogue animal got onto his ranch. While Rick was confident it had truly never gotten near his cattle, the government shut down his operation. He was quarantined for six months to ensure the health of his stock. During this time, he had no income coming in but he had to maintain the usual expense of caring for the livestock and running the business.

When the quarantine came to an end, he was so cash strapped, he would have had a difficult time continuing the business, had he wanted to. Those two bad experiences so close together left him simply wanting out. With his business back in his hands, he took an offer to sell the ranch.

Around the same time, the issue of Mad Cow Disease was sweeping the news so his secondary business, a packing plant, was also suffering. He decided to further liquidate his holdings, and he sold the packing plant as well.

While he had gotten past his financial woes, the sale of his two businesses left him without a job. He wasn't ready for retirement so he began to look into what he could do.

Always entrepreneurial, he began to explore the idea of beef jerky. Running his various businesses over the years meant Rick did a lot of traveling. As he would crisscross America, he often found himself pulling off the beaten path to mom and pop stores in small towns. It was at these types of stores where he would inevitably find a locally made beef jerky.

Though inconsistent in quality and taste, he found out the locally made products were clearly better than the national brands. The big names in the jerky world, the ones found at the nationally known convenience markets, seemed to more closely resemble science projects than a meat product.

While he had made a habit of trying new jerky products, the best he could find he would rate as palatable. He never was successful in finding one which resembled a jerky he would offer if he had made it himself.

With Rick now not working, but actively seeking a new opportunity, he began to think about what if he could make his own beef jerky? Could he, in fact, deliver a product which was better than the local brands he found in Small Town America? (He knew he could easily outdo the big names, but the smaller brands would be the key here).

On the positive side, he did know the meat industry well. He knew the standards for meat handling and preparation. He was versed in the rules and regulations. He even had contacts who could be of use in getting started. He liked the idea of a product which wasn't as time sensitive or which you had to have special equipment to deliver (like some of his rancher friends who had started milk businesses).

Knowing the problems he had gone through in ranching, he didn't want a consumer product which was particularly sensitive. With a stable shelf life, no need for special equipment to deliver, and little health concerns when the proper preparation procedures are followed to prepare, Rick thought jerky fit the bill perfectly for a possible entrée back into entrepreneurship.

The downside for him was he simply didn't have any experience at all in this area. He had never owned a consumer goods business. He had never been on the retail side of the food business. Furthermore, he had never even made beef jerky.

After careful contemplation and consultation with his wife Ellen, he decided to give it a try. He would work the production/distribution side of the business, and Ellen was going to focus on the development of the recipes. Their first product was a no-brainer for them. Their son-in-law was a green chili farmer, so they decided to go with a green chili jerky.

The company name was vital in selling and marketing the product. Rick and Ellen's Beef Jerky just didn't pop. Rick decided to go with a nickname he had always called his father: Fatman's. In the Robey family, this wasn't a derogatory statement; it was a term of endearment. He had always just referred to his father as "Fatman" and now he was going to name the company after his dad.

With his father's blessing (he has since passed away but was proud Rick named the company after him), Rick and Ellen started Fatman's Beef Jerky. Not coming from the packaged consumer goods business, Rick was taken off-guard to find that having a superior product does not buy you inroads with the staple of beef jerky retail sales: convenience store owners.

The nationally-affiliated convenience stores are so tied into the jerky megabrands, they won't even consider adding a new product to the mix. A superior brand is actually looked down upon as it may impact sales of the national brand, which offer rebates and incentives serving as contracts to hold shelf space.

With no ability to break through the wall the national brands have firmly established, Rick was delegated to the local mom and pop stores where the national jerky brands didn't have contracts. Even though they liked Rick's product based upon the fact it sold for them, their volume was too low to really make Rick very successful. He had to go a different direction if he wanted to keep Fatman's going.

One day Rick was sharing the story of the difficulties he was having getting a footing for his product in gas stations and convenience stores with a friend. His buddy, a hardware store owner, stated, "Bring some to me, I can sell it for you."

With two years of banging on door with little to show for it, Rick was more than willing to try anything so he set up a display at his friend's hardware store. If nothing else, he felt at least there certainly wasn't anything else like it in the store.

Almost immediately, it began to sell. His buddy took note that not only was it selling well, he had customers coming to his store to look specifically for his jerky. Rick's product was actually driving traffic to the store. In retail, driving foot traffic is the golden goose. If your product can get 'em in the doors, you've locked yourself onto those shelves as a manufacturer.

Rick took this experience and began to actively market almost exclusively to hardware stores. The name was often an icebreaker to garner their interest. Then he could tell the story of the success he had bringing customers to other stores.

Rick's packaging was also helping sell it to hardware store buyers and the public. He had actively avoided making his product look flashy or overdesigned. He kept it simple with color-coded labels and clear packaging so people could see his product. It screamed homemade, and people could see the quality he was offering via the clear package.

With the catchy name, simple package and superior product, the story stayed the same the more stores he got it in: Fatman's Beef Jerky brings customers to your store. Soon, he was working with the top 10 hardware chains/co-ops in the United States.

He no longer even tries to get into the gas stations and convenience stores. This makes him a valuable partner for the hardware stores he is working with as it remains the only place customers can buy it. They can't pop into the corner gas station; they need to go to the local hardware store. Once they are there, they may need to pick up a few other things as well. It ends up being a winning formula for everyone involved.

Today, he offers 14 different flavors in various levels of heat. His wife Ellen continues to actively work on new flavors. Some immediately are hits; others take some time to take hold, and still others never quite make it. They tried a honey garlic, but the combination just never smelled right in the package, and they had a dill pickle flavor that tasted great but the vinegar always ended up drying the meat out too much. Overall, they have always ended up with more winners than losers.

Rick notes that one of the greatest differences between the cattle business and the consumer goods business is the use of contracts. In the cattle business, your word was your honor and handshake deal was almost all you ever needed.

A contract was to only write down what was agreed to in a handshake agreement. The food business means he's managing contracts for almost every aspect of his business.

That small difference aside, Rick seems to have found a way to utilize the business skills he honed his whole life to apply to his jerky business. With a solid chain of distribution now entrenched, and plenty of room to keep growing, the future of Fatman's Beef Jerky looks extremely bright.

Fatman would be proud!

Fatman's Beef Jerky Photo Album

Rick and Ellen Robey

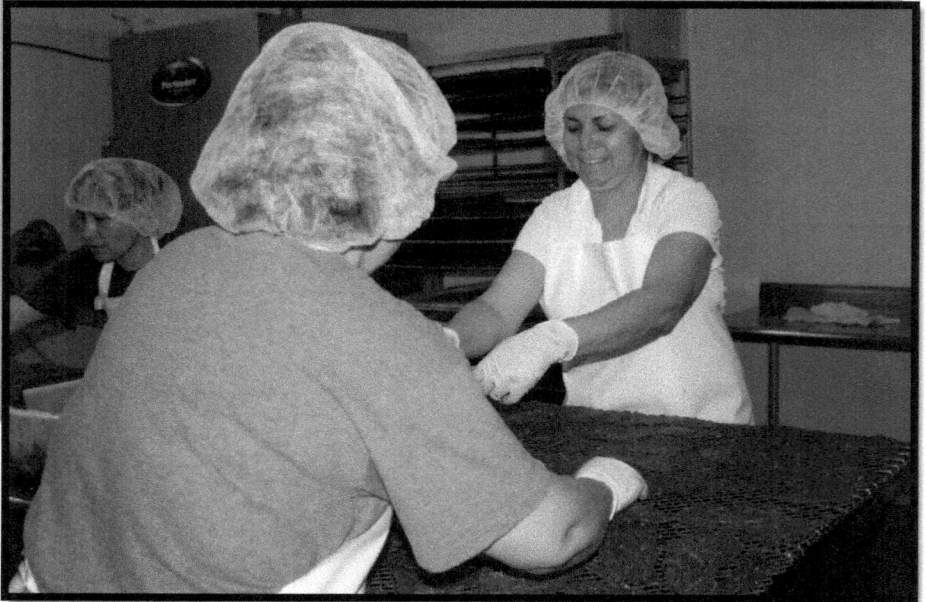

Making a batch of beef jerky

Beef jerky on the rack, ready to bag

Introducing Fatman's to potential customers at a trade show

Product detail

Fatman's product lineup

Chapter 4: Beer
Great Divide Brewing Co.

2201 Arapahoe Street
Denver, CO 80205
(303) 296 - 9640

greatdivide.com
info@greatdivide.com

Established
1994

Leadership
Brian Dunn, Founder/President

Products
More than a dozen year round beers and an additional dozen, or so, seasonal/specialty/limited release beers

Wanna split a four of Yeti?…

Hobby brewing.

That's where the story always starts with beer. Brian Dunn's story isn't any different in that regard. He was a hobby brewer, but it takes a little more interesting turn than your typical basement to storefront operation.

Brian was born and grew up in Vermont. Later in his childhood he lived in Ohio before attending college at Colorado State University. At C.S.U. he studied Soil Science and Agriculture. He put his degree to work helping out others. He spent five years overseas helping build farms and irrigation systems.

His travels took him to over 35 countries. During these trips, he would spend his down time learning the local take on one of his favorite passions: brewing. He always like to check out the local beer scene in the places he visited and try to learn as much as he could about the techniques and ingredients, which made the area's brewed beers unique.

After coming back to the United States, he returned to Colorado and went to back to school at the University of Denver. During the course of his studies, he wrote a marketing and sales plan for a proposed beer company.

While in graduate school, he decided farming wasn't his future. He wanted to turn his hobby into his full-time job after graduation. He decided to put together a full business plan which assisted him in securing the funding he needed to start the Great Divide Brewing Co. Brian was successful in securing a series of loans from friends, family, associates and a loan from the city of Denver to make this happen.

Going from a hobby brewer to launching a beer brand is a big undertaking. Many individuals spend years with apprenticeships, taking classes and getting advice from other craft brewers.

Not Brian Dunn. He just jumped right in and elected to learn the business on the go. Brian started out as a one-person company. He would literally get going between 2 and 3 every morning, starting out brewing until about 9:00 a.m. He then went to work selling and delivering his product.

The drivers for most people - money and success - eluded him initially. What kept him going during those early years was the fun of it all.

He found companies to be standoffish when he came in with his beer. He was able to win them over by talking about the fact it was a local product, and this wasn't a beer made by some giant corporation… he was the guy actually brewing it.

Colorado offered him a large advantage over many states in that he was allowed to sell his own product. Most states require beer companies to use a distributor to sell their products to retailers. This law allowed Brian to have those great sales calls where he was introducing himself as the salesperson/delivery person/brewer/customer service and owner. It truly made for some really great interactions and experiences with potential customers!

Offering taste tests was the final quotient to securing a prospects' business. Once he got a potential buyer to actually taste his beer, he knew he was "in."

Even with a standout product, a great story behind it and his unique sales approach, he was stretched to the limits on time. The best he was managing to do during his first five years was to get by. His goal was to get the company profitable before taking a salary himself.

As sales started to grow, he began to add staff and expand his product line. One of Great Divide's signature marketing strategies was to utilize bold names and fun and memorable graphics on its labels. Names like Titan IPA (their bestselling beer today), Yeti, Hercules Double IPA, Wolfgang, Nomad, Hoss, Claymore Scotch Ale, Colette, Denver Pale Ale, Nomad, Hades and Lasso became part of their product lineup.

With its sasquatch theme, The Yeti Imperial Stout is an advertiser's dream. Highly marketable, the Yeti silhouette is also incorporated into branding in other offerings as well: a Chocolate Oak Aged, an Espresso Oak Aged and an Oatmeal Imperial Stout.

From the beginning, the company has been bestowed with industry awards. By 1997 Great Divide began collecting awards from the Great American Beer Festival™. Currently, they are at 18 and counting. Additionally, they also have five of the prestigious World Beer Cup™ awards.

One of the biggest indicators the company had made it didn't come from an award, but instead inclusion in the product offerings at Invesco Field™, the home of the Denver Broncos™. Great Divide Brewing Company was one of only three craft brewers selling their product at Broncos™ games when the stadium opened in 2001.

Today, Great Divide offers a welcoming atmosphere at its company headquarters in Denver. Visitors can take tours of the facility seven days a week where they can learn about company history and see the production process live. Guests can sample beer and buy packaged beer and gifts on site as well.

Brian keeps the future goals for the company very simple: Great Divide Brewing Co. will strive to continue to make better beers. He hopes to accomplish this by continuing to learn about new and better processes and ingredients and making his company a fun place to work, which is staffed with great people.

A typical day for Brian today is almost as busy as he was when he started the company 20 years ago. Now, rather than being involved in every step of brewing, selling and distributing his beer, he's deeply involved in the inner-workings of an expanding corporation. Regular responsibilities for Brian include marketing, branding, human resources, distributor interaction and overseeing construction projects.

Yep, it sounds like he's keeping to the hard work approach which got him to where he is at today!

Great Divide Brewing Co. Photo Album

Brian Dunn

Brian Dunn… havin' fun!

The first fermenters in 1994

The Great Divide team, Christmas 1994

Anybody bring a tap?

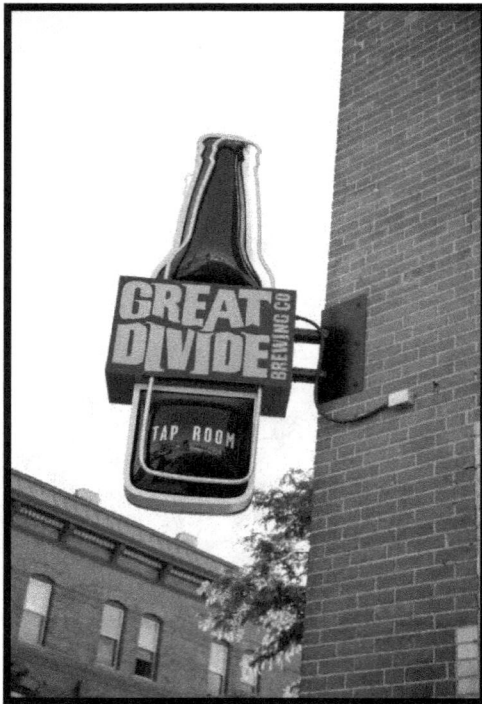

The sign outside the brewery

Brian serving up a beer in the tap room in 1994

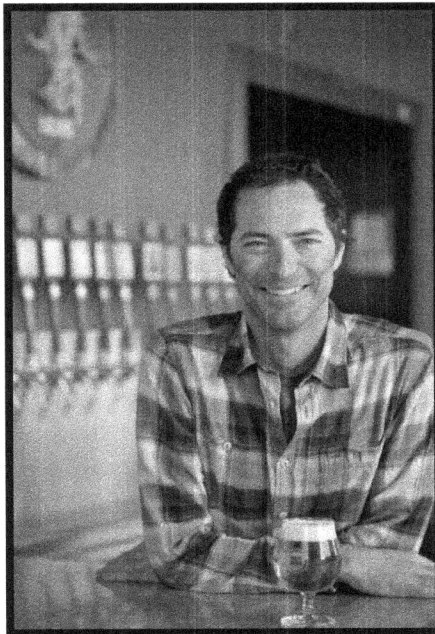
Brian in the tap room today

Product Packaging Detail

Great Divide product lineup

Chapter 5: Caramels
Jonboy Caramels

Seattle, WA

jonboycaramels.com
info@jonboycaramels.com

Established
2009

Leadership
Jonathan Sue and Jason Alm, Co-Owners

Products
Flavored caramels

$300 + $300…

When you look back at the lives of two people involved in a joint venture, you realize had there been one slight twist in the life of even one of them, the product they have created likely never would have been made. It's almost definitely the case with Jonboy Caramels. Owners Jon Sue and Jason Alm possess two unique skill sets, and each of their lives involved several relocations until they both ended up in Seattle where they would rekindle a friendship and ultimately start their business.

The Creative One
Jon Sue lived in both Idaho and Montana before he made his way to Seattle. As a hobby, he enjoyed working with different ingredients in the kitchen. It was one of his creative treats which would serve as the kickstarter for getting the company going. For Christmas of 2008, he made a batch of caramels he gave as gifts to friends and family.

Prior to Jonboy caramels, Jon's career path had been more traditional than his business partner Jason, having worked his way from a store level position at Whole Foods® to a marketing position at their regional office.

The Entrepreneur
Jason Alm also moved around several times before landing in Seattle. He had lived outside of Chicago growing up. In college he moved to Flagstaff, Arizona, where he studied hotel and restaurant management. He worked in Colorado for a short time after graduation and then made his way back to Arizona for a stint prior to making the move to Seattle.

By the time he ended up in Seattle, Jason realized the hotel and restaurant business wasn't for him. He began working in construction, but he wanted to start his own business so he opened a tile installation company.

It takes a lot of coincidences for two strangers, to start a business together and the story of Jonboy Caramels is no exception. When Jon's sister married Jason's brother, these two Seattle residents were introduced.

This could have been the end of the tale, but Jason happened to be on Jon's distribution list when he gave out the boxes of his homemade caramels for Christmas of 2008.

Jon, the creative one, viewed them as an extension of himself and a way to connect with friends and family at the holidays. Jason, the entrepreneur, viewed them entirely differently. He saw them as a potential business.

They were better than anything he had ever tasted. They were made by Jon on his own at his house. Couldn't the two work together, scale up a little, and have a nice little side business which had the opportunity to bring in a little cash?

Jason approached Jon about going into business with the caramels. They both had jobs and would keep them. This venture was going to be a 10 – 15 hours a week side-gig which could potentially fulfill the creative and entrepreneurial sides of each of them. Jason spoke of the Seattle food scene and how people support local companies. He went on about the caramels Jon made and how much better they were than anything you could find on the market.

Jon liked Jason's ideas for the business, and they decided to start working together. They pooled the capital they believed they would need to get off of the ground. The investment was $300 apiece.

After much thought of what to call their caramel company, a sibling of Jon's suggested they name it Jonboy Caramels after Jon's childhood nickname. Jason and Jon both liked the name. It was simple and easy to remember, yet it seemed to transcend simply being a person's name and convey the fact these were homemade treats, made with care by real people and not some mass produced candy confection.

Having already started a tile business, Jason took care of the licensing and registration needs of the company. Jon was to handle the recipes and the cooking. They found some packaging which fit into their budget, and they went to work.

When they had their first batch of caramels ready to go, they targeted the local and popular Ballard Farmers Market™ to sell their product. They had a problem; there weren't any spots open for them at the time. They kept bringing samples to the management until one day they were called to inform them there was a cancellation. They could get in if they were able to get there right away. Jason and Jon made it and set up shop.

They sold out their entire inventory in 90 minutes.

Those 90 minutes took the hyphen right out of Jonboy Caramels' moniker. No longer were they a "hobbyists-business," they were now officially a "business-business," or as it is officially and conventionally known, simply a "business."

They invested all of the proceeds right back into the company. They also moved out of Jon's kitchen and began cooking at a shared community commercial kitchen. Soon, their production needs were taking all of the free time available at the kitchen so they opened up their own facility where they could run production as much as they needed to meet demand.

The housing crash never hit Seattle like it did the rest of the country. The reverberations did eventually cause a slowdown for the Seattle market. By 2009, Jason's tile installation had really started to grind to a halt.

It actually worked out okay for him because it allowed him to focus more time on Jonboy Caramels. One day, when he looked at the books and realized he didn't have any upcoming jobs, he simply decided to close the tile business and focus exclusively on growing Jonboy Caramels. Paying more attention to Jonboy could only help them realize their long-term goals for the company.

Most of the focus for Jonboy Caramels was to increase production and get out into the community via more appearances at farmers' markets. Their reasons for participating in the markets go well beyond simply what they sell while they are set-up there. Jonboy Caramels had developed into an "event candy:"

Hosting a party… have a bowl of Jonboy Caramels.

Invited to a party… bring Jonboy Caramels.

Want awesome guest favors at your wedding… Jonboy Caramels will make for a memorable treat.

Individuals being introduced to Jonboy at the farmers' markets would not only give them orders for their events, the guests at these events often turned out to be future customers for Jonboy as well.

Introductions at farmers' markets also led to most of the P.R. they have received and even had been their entrée into the stores they are working with. They are just starting to actively pursue new wholesale opportunities with retailers. Up until now, all of the stores Jonboy Caramels had been in came through the stores contacting them - most buyer interaction came at… you guessed it: farmers' markets.

The most rewarding part for Jonboy Caramels has been to simply see how the idea of a Christmas gift could be turned into a company. Not through the investment of tens of thousands of dollars… simply through a quality product and the hard work and tenacity it takes to get it on the market.

The future for Jonboy Caramels is to do what they are doing, just do it on a bigger scale. The model for success is already established. They just need to be involved in more events and secure placement in more stores. They recently took a step towards their goal by adding a small, but nationwide retailer to the mix.

It is deals like those which will help Jonboy Caramels take the final step on their journey from hobbyists-business, to business to finally: BUSINESS!

Luckily, the stars were aligned, and those series of random events brought "the creative one" and "the entrepreneur" together so we can all enjoy a box of Jonboy Caramels.

Jonboy Caramels Photo Album

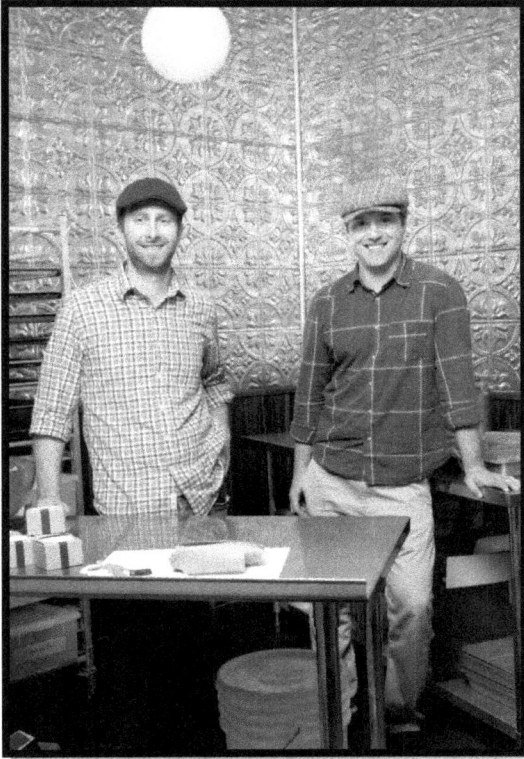

Jason Alm and Jon Sue

Bowl full of caramels

At a farmers' market

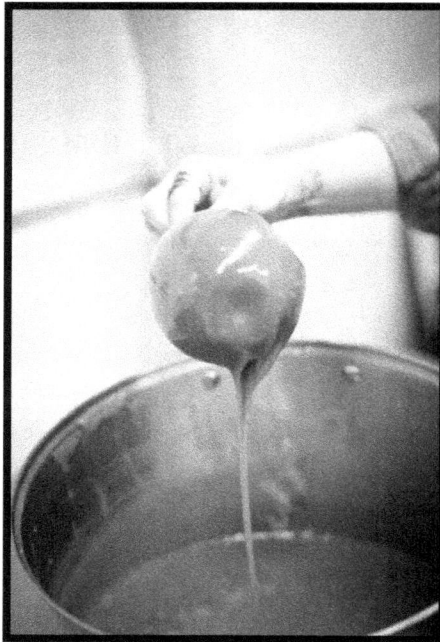

Now that's a caramel apple

Jonboy's sign at Whole Foods®

Cut caramels

Loose caramels

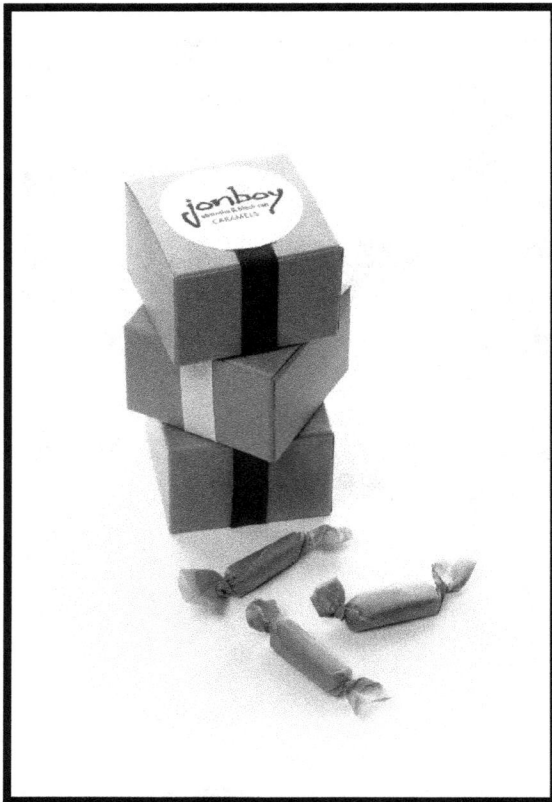

Jonboy Caramel product lineup

Chapter 6: Frozen Pizza
Mystic Pizza Company

Elk Grove Village, IL
(847) 378 - 8221

mysticpizza.com
apawlis@mysticpizza.com

Established
2012

Leadership
Patrick J. "P.J." Pawlis, General Manager

Products
Frozen pizza in the following toppings: Cheese, Ultimate Pepperoni, House Special, Spinach, Margherita, Buffalo Style Chicken, Italian Sausage, Three Meat and Roasted Vegetable

Yes, it's that Mystic Pizza...

If you took a random poll and asked people what is the most famous Steakhouse in the United States was, you would have some serious debate. Such Travel Channel™/Food Network™ favorites as Peter Luger™ in New York, St. Elmos™ in Indianapolis or Dickie Brenan's™ in New Orleans would be bound to show up. There is also a large contingent who would go the route of offering up the celebrity steakhouses. Names like Michael Jordan's, Mike Ditka's or Brett Favre's would make more than a few lists. The final contingent would be those who favor the gastrointestinal challenges of a food competition. Undoubtedly, the 72 oz. steak challenge from the Big Texan™ in Amarillo, Texas, would make its way into the debate as well.

If you transitioned to burgers, the drivers of the debate would be the burgers themselves. They almost become some sort of pseudo-celebrities which fans create bucket lists looking to check them off by name. Think along the lines of the "Juicy Lucy" from Matt's Bar™ in Minneapolis, the "Thurman Burger" from Thurman's Café™ in Columbus, Ohio, "The Original Burger" from Louis' Lunch™ in New Haven, Connecticut, or the famously Saturday Night Live-parodied "Cheezborger-Cheezborger" from the Billy Goat Tavern™ in Chicago.

Pizza is different. Despite the fact it may exceed any other category of food in popularity, if you throw out the chains, there are really only three challengers for the acknowledgement of the most famous pizza parlor in the United States, and in reality, there is one clear-cut winner.

The first name to come up is always Ray's in New York. The problem is there are dozens of pizza parlors in New York, all with some stake to being the original or the best Ray's pizza and debate rages amongst fans as to which one is the best.

The second contender is Pizzaland™ in North Arlington, New Jersey. Any fanatic of the HBO™ TV show The Sopranos™ remembers Pizzaland™ from its opening credits. Admittedly,

Pizzaland™ does have some great pizza. The problem is only truly rabid fans even pick up on Pizzaland's™ inclusion in the show since they only are shown briefly in the opening credits. A few episodes go on location to a pizza parlor, but it's simply referred to as "the pizza parlor" on the show and not necessarily as Pizzaland™, so there isn't necessarily the true connection which makes everyone who has watched the show think of them if they were debating the notion of the most famous pizza parlor in the United States.

Eliminating the bevy of Ray's in New York and Pizzaland™ from New Jersey means there is one clear-cut winner as to the most famous pizza parlor in the United States, and it's Mystic Pizza™ in Mystic, Connecticut.

Known for a great pie, the restaurant served as the backdrop for Julia Robert's first feature film, 1988's **Mystic Pizza**. Despite an accomplished career which includes feature roles in dozens of notable movies, Golden Globes™ and Oscar™ awards, total box office receipts amongst the highest of any actor in the business, **Mystic Pizza** remains one of her quintessential roles. It was a low budget, coming-of-age film which resonated with an audience and serves as one of the movies used to define the 1980s.

Opened in 1973 by the Zelepos family in the vacation community of Mystic Connecticut, the pizza parlor was famous for serving up great pizzas long before the movie was shot on location there. It's true, with its famously delicious pizza, and a tie-in to a great movie which featured the debut of one of Hollywood's favorite actresses, Mystic Pizza is clearly the winner of the debate of the most famous pizza parlor in the United States.

When you consider how iconic the brand is, it's almost amazing to think how it literally fell in the lap of P.J. Pawlis.

Mystic Pizza, the frozen pizza line with the same name as the famous restaurant, was started by none other than Christo

Zelepos, the owner of the newly bestowed by **Small Brand America**, "Most Famous Pizza Parlor in the United States." He utilized the same fresh ingredients, techniques and spices to create his frozen pizza as he did in his restaurant.

While Christo was making his famous pies in Mystic, 900 miles away in Chicago, P.J. Pawlis' father was in the frozen food business. A Korean War veteran, he initially was in the food manufacturing industry with a line of Polish products he made and sold. After transitioning out of that business, he went into frozen food distribution and over the years he acquired and sold a few companies.

When he retired, he sold off his company, and P.J. went to work for the company which had acquired his father's old company.

Around this same time, Mystic Pizza, the frozen pizza line, had changed hands a few times. Christo Zelepos had sold it, and it became a line in multi-brand frozen food conglomerate's book of business. The company where P.J. had worked made an acquisition, and Mystic Pizza was included in their catalog.

Knowing the quality of the brand, the power of the famous name, and it's multitude of tie-ins to consumers' psyche, P.J. acquired it himself and began to work to make the frozen food line as famous as the fresh pizza still being served in the restaurant.

The start to a great product was there: the name, the quality ingredients (whole milk mozzarella versus the partial skim milk most frozen pizza utilize), and the taste (the garlic sauce made famous at the restaurant with their notable spices). The product line, featuring nine pizzas, was pretty diversified. There were classic offerings (cheese, three meat and pepperoni) but there were also specialty pizzas (buffalo chicken, margherita, spinach) and four which were all-natural vegetarian offerings, meaning the line appeals to everyone who likes pizza. (That literally is everybody, isn't it?)

Make no mistake there was work which needed to be done. The product was being marketed as a 10" pizza, which ends up being too big for a single serving pizza, yet too small for multi-serving. The label graphics were bad, and distribution was confined mostly to the Northeast.

P.J. changed the size to an 11½" pie, he reshot the graphics and on January 1, 2013, he re-launched the brand with a goal of making it a household name.

P.J. started by working to increase distribution in the Northeast, which was the backyard of the restaurant and in his hometown of Chicago. Dealing with the traditional obstacles of the grocery industry (limited shelf space with charges to get in the door) has made it a challenge but his hands-on approach of personally calling on buyers, sharing samples, and getting the brand name out there, has helped. He has gone from no distribution in Chicago to shelf space in over 200 stores in a little over a year. Wal-Mart® has been supportive of his efforts and is looking to bring him onboard in 2015 in the Midwest.

He has plans to continue to grow distribution in the Midwest and may add additional product lines. He has already started work on a microwave product line, and an organic pizza could possibly be in the mix down the road as well.

Despite the fact Mystic Pizza™, the restaurant, and Mystic Pizza, the frozen food pizza are not affiliated businesses anymore, they still have a great relationship. P.J. maintains a personal friendship with Christo Zelepos and stops by to see him anytime he is in the Northeast. Both men also realize the importance of co-branding. Every pizza bought at the restaurant is an advertisement for the frozen food brand and vice-versa so they continue to acknowledge one another as partners. The restaurant and the frozen pizzas still share the web domain of *mysticpizza.com*. There is a landing page where you can then enter either Christo's restaurants (he even has a second Mystic

Pizza™ location now) or select the frozen pizza line owned by P.J. Pawlis.

Now, if Julia Roberts would just make a *Mystic Pizza II*, P.J.'s job would likely get a lot easier!

Mystic Pizza Photo Album

P.J. Pawlis

P.J.'s father Ron Pawlis

P.J.'s daughter Ashley

In-store demo

Out of pizza, again!

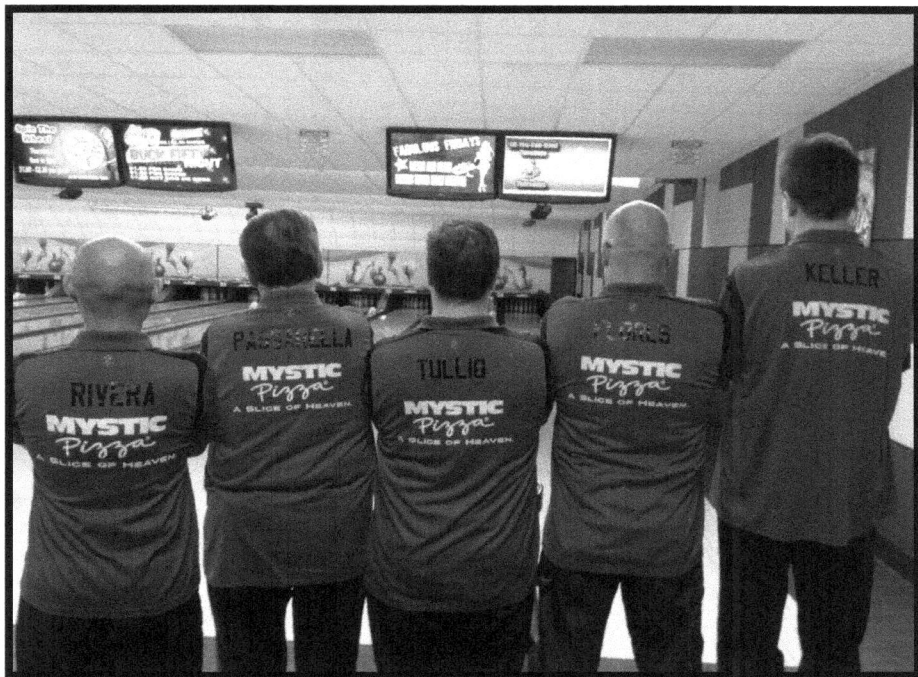

The Mystic Pizza bowling team

The final product

Mystic Pizza product lineup

Chapter 7: Granola
Upfront Foods, LLC

Boca Raton, FL
(561) 886 - 0209

upfrontfoods.com
info@upfrontfoods.com

Established
2010

Leadership
Gigi Twist, Founder/President

Products
Granola in three flavors: Straight Up Granola, Straight Up Granola with Cranberries and Nutty Granola

Brought to you by the greatest name in the food industry…

The name Upfront Foods is pretty special in that it encompasses a simple, yet memorable company brand/name, it is a descriptor of their corporate mantra (being "up front" with customers about their food choices by using simple ingredients with no additives or preservatives), and is even a marketing tool which is utilized in their packaging. The front panel of Upfront Foods packaging contains ingredient and nutritional information… something which is always left to the back or bottom of the packages on consumer brands. Upfront Foods' story of 7 simple ingredients in their signature granola is so important, it has to be told on the front of the package.

Even still, Upfront Foods isn't the greatest name in the food industry. Yes, it's in the running for sure, but this designation doesn't belong to a company; it actually belongs to a person. That's right, the greatest name in the food industry is none other than the owner of Upfront Foods: Gigi Twist.

Gigi and her husband Eddie grew up in the same eastern Arkansas town. They married, and she became a school teacher while her husband was a farmer. As early as the '70s and '80s when Gigi was teaching, she witnessed firsthand the need for the product she would one day create. Kids simply didn't have healthy snack choices available to them at that time. Most children were snacking on chips or candy between meals at school.

While you may be able to look back and realize the seeds of what would become Upfront Foods may have been planted while Gigi was teaching, she certainly wasn't aware of it. She didn't fashion herself as the entrepreneurial type. She never desired to have an ownership or leadership stake in an organization. She was fulfilled and very content teaching children remedial math and reading.

A business opportunity took Gigi and Eddie to Boca Raton, Florida where they both worked in traditional business/office jobs. Gigi stayed on until 1997 when she retired. From 1997 – 2010, she enjoyed retired life getting more involved in her church and having lunches with friends, and taking it easy.

She also had some health issues and when a doctor encouraged her to watch what she was eating, she started reading labels more than she had in the past (those seeds planted when she was teaching were starting to germinate). She was often amazed to find products labeled "healthy" or "heart-healthy" were packed with additives and ingredients which she had no idea what they actually were.

With snacking choices she felt were less than desirable at the store, she started baking her own granola snacks. Friends and family enjoyed them as much as she did so she would give them as gifts or bake some for special requests (seeds in full bloom now).

In 2010 she thought there was one more chapter to be written in her life story so she decided to go back to work. Initially, she thought she might go back to her passion and something which had been important in her life for a long time: teaching. After a 3-month internship, she realized the industry had changed a lot since she was away.

Having missed the integration of computers into the classroom during her first turn as a teacher, Gigi really didn't like the idea of learning the various systems required for the now omnipresent computers used inside the classroom for lesson planning, teaching tools and even for grades and interaction with parents. She decided if there was to be one more chapter of her life, teaching wasn't going to be it.

When she began to explore the idea of turning her hobby granola into a business, she had two independent recommendations for the same culinary nutritionist. Starting out with an expert was just what Gigi needed. She was able to learn her home-baked granola, while delicious, contained 16 grams of fat per serving. She needed to refine her recipe, scale it up for mass production, all while maintaining a commitment to nutrition, simple ingredients and taste.

Once the process was complete, Gigi had exactly what she was looking for. Her ingredients list didn't read like a science experiment. It was seven simple elements people could relate to and understand.

Gigi's next plan was to find a co-packer to recreate her recipe, cook and package it for her. Her naiveté in regard to the grocery industry left her believing this is how the system worked. You develop a great product, you prepare and package it, and then you sell it. Without a path to market, Gigi struggled selling her product a case at a time, always trying to stay a step ahead of product expiration dates.

With the expense of the added layer of the co-packer and lack of a "go-to-market" plan, Gigi decided to hit the start over button. She hired a consultant with knowledge of the grocery business. In the summer of 2011, she opened a manufacturing and warehouse center in Boca Raton. Through the assistance of her consultant, she had a clear strategy to go to market with distributors and food brokers introducing her product to major chains.

She also guided her brand through the arduous process of becoming both "Certified Vegan" as well as "Certified Non-GMO." Both of these steps opened her up to groups who seek out these certifications.

Today, she remains committed to keeping it simple and remaining up front with her customers. She still uses the same seven ingredients as the basis for her granola: oats, maple syrup, brown sugar, canola oil, sea salt, flax seed and orange peel powder. She adds sliced and sweetened cranberries to her fruit mix and pecans and almonds to her nut mixture.

She is pleased to note her customer base is pretty diverse. She has a large contingent of healthy and active-lifestyle buyers.

She certainly has the individuals who shop for vegan and non-GMO products. She has also been pleased to find moms buying her product for school lunches and snacks. (If she ever writes a book, the story of her initial desire to offer children healthy alternatives certainly has come full-circle.)

Gigi has found the most surprising buyers are office workers. While you may not initially view people sitting in cubicles at their desk all day as those seeking particularly healthy snacks, but then again, like the school kids, they need healthy choices… without recess, maybe even more than the kids! She is pleased to be able to offer better choices for those 10:00 a.m. or 3:00 p.m. munchies attacks. (This certainly seems like a better plan than checking out the company calendar to see who's birthday it is to score a piece of cake or some cookies.)

There has even been some personal betterment for Gigi as she's continued on this journey. Once technology adverse, she's now running her company and utilizing the computer more than ever before. She's even actively involved in social media with much of the company's marketing coming through interaction with customers via Facebook® and Twitter®.

Long-term, she believes there is room to expand Upfront Foods. As they build up a loyal customer base, there very well may be opportunities for line extensions. As they continue to build customer's trust, it makes sense for other products like bread, cookies or savory snacks to be made under the Upfront Foods name. Gigi is willing to venture into these other lines so long as she can continue offering items made in a similar manner as her granola: simple ingredients which consumer can understand and trust as healthy alternatives to flavors created in a lab.

Gigi's daughter Kaki (a nickname from her birth name of Catherine - the Twist family is apparently committed to memorable names) insisted her mother go with her lifelong nickname of Gigi over her own birth name of Glenda as the listed owner of the company.

Gigi thought she may be better suited to go with her legal name so she might be perceived as more professional. Kaki was insistent that the name Gigi Twist was like a brand by itself. People will not forget you when you introduce yourself to them as Gigi Twist. As a person who is meeting people and trying to get her product to market, this is a valuable resource.

It begs the question, why go with Upfront Foods? How did this company not become Gigi Twist's Twisted Granola, or something similar?

Gigi sums it up best by saying, "I didn't want customers or potential store buyers to think they were buying a product made by a stripper."

Touché.

Upfront Foods it is!

Upfront Foods Photo Album

Gigi Twist

Upfront Foods' shelf display (notice the ingredients and nutrition facts on the front of the packaging, not just a name, they are "upfront" in every way with their customers)

Gigi's role takes her from making granola...

...to office duties (pictured with her husband Eddie)

Granola production

Filling the granola bags

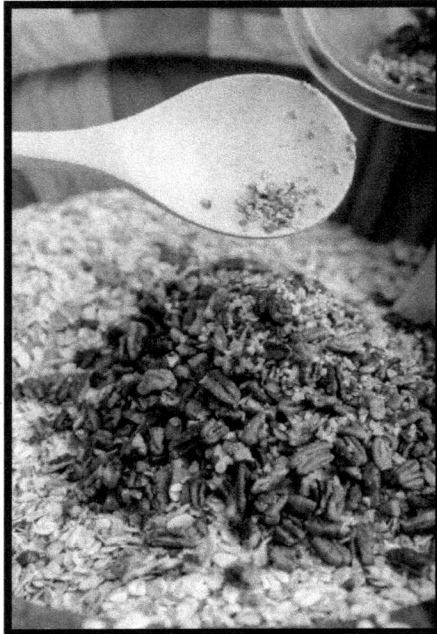

Only natural ingredients go into Upfront Foods' products

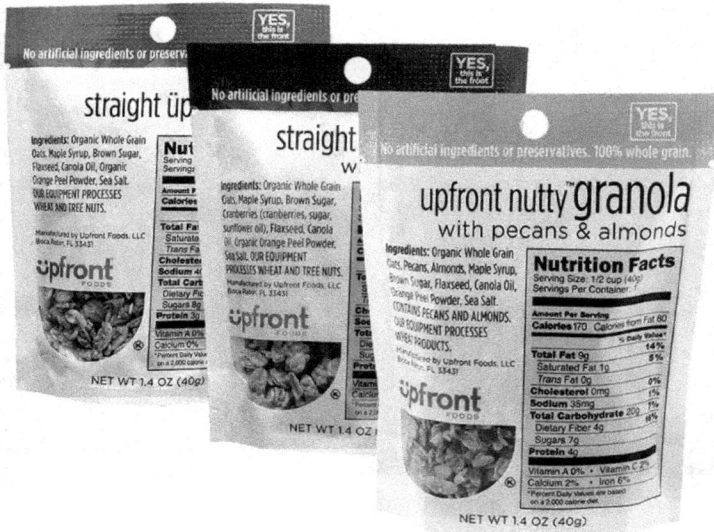

Upfront Foods' product lineup

Chapter 8: Grilling Sauces & Gourmet Products
Tennessee Gourmet

"When You're Ready For Something Different"®
Tennessee
Gourmet®

Mount Juliet, TN
(800) 360-6345

tngourmetsauce.com
tnsauce@bellsouth.net

Established
2002

Leadership
Sue Sykes, Owner & President

Products
Grilling sauce under the name Tennessee Gourmet and Tasty Cookin' as well as cheese spread, spices, salad dressing, jelly and habanero extract

For all of your telecommunications, gardening and gourmet food needs…

There tends to be a distinction between individuals who work corporate jobs and entrepreneurs. Those lines blur a little with Sue Sykes, her husband and business partner Gary Dummer and their friend and fellow business partner Tom Ellison.

The three met working at a large telecommunications company. Over time, they worked together, or for one another, in a variety of capacities with careers spanning 25 – 30 years. In 2001, the company began to experience some financial difficulties. With the economy struggling and the company following suit, it began to offer early retirement packages.

During their careers they combined for over 5,000,000 airline miles and now each was ready for a change. All three took the packages and began to seek their next adventure. Rather than getting back into the corporate grind, they explored how they could continue to work together and utilize the retirement packages to start their own business.

Their first foray into entrepreneurship began with a gardening company called Green Genes, Inc. They all enjoyed working in the garden as a hobby and turning it into a business seemed like a natural.

Three retirees running a gardening/landscaping company was a great stopgap solution, but long-term they realized the back-breaking work associated with Green Genes wouldn't be something they could do forever. While continuing to manage the landscaping company, they started developing some of Sue's homemade sauce recipes.

Sue had always enjoyed developing her own sauces and spice mixtures, but turning it into a business would present numerous challenges. First and foremost was the need for a commercial kitchen to prepare the product. Without access to a facility where they could prepare the sauces on their own, they would have to use a co-packer.

This not only adds an additional layer of cost, it also increases the inventory they would need on-hand since the co-packers required minimum runs which far exceeded what a typical start-up would be willing to make.

With Sue refining her recipes through trial, error and taste tests on friends and family, the three searched for an alternative to the utilization of a co-packer. It proved to be a much greater challenge than they initially anticipated. Not wanting to invest in a full-time commercial facility, they sought out a community kitchen which could be rented as needed.

The trio found an individual at the local Department of Agriculture willing to help them. With the assistance of former State Representative Stratton Bone, the Tennessee Department of Agriculture, the USDA/Rural Development, the Wilson County School System, and a lot of sweat equity, they were able to secure a publicly and privately funded community kitchen. The Cumberland Culinary Center™ at Cumberland University was born in 2010.

Now, they were officially in business making their Tennessee Gourmet products in batch sizes that were appropriate for a new company just getting started. This also opened up another opportunity for the group. Cumberland University sought assistance in managing the facility.

In addition to the landscaping company and the sauces, the group now would assume the responsibilities of managing the operation of the Cumberland Culinary Center™. The responsibilities include instructing individuals on the proper use of the equipment, cleaning and sanitizing all machinery and ensuring everything is in working order and managing the schedule.

Their contact at the Tennessee Department of Agriculture also proved invaluable in garnering the attention of the grocery industry. The Tennessee Department of Agriculture maintains a group called Pick Tennessee™ which promotes local agriculture and supports products made in Tennessee.

At a Pick Tennessee™ food show, they made contact with an individual who got their Tennessee Gourmet sauces into Whole Foods®.

With the success they were experiencing with their grilling sauces, they began to expand the company by offering other product lines. Gary began to formulate some jellies. A salad dressing, dipping sauces, spice line and a cheese spread were also introduced.

Many of their products feature heat scales with fun names which start with an "S" as a nod to Sue. For instance, their grilling sauce comes in four levels of heat:

Sensible – No heat

Sneaky Hot – Just a little heat

Silly Hot – Four times the heat of Sneaky Hot

Stupid Hot – Six times the heat of Sneaky Hot

Fans of their products have begun to expect these fun scales so they continue it with every offering with different levels of heat (using different names/like Snappy and Snappy Hot for their pepper jelly).

While they do some advertising in Tennessee-based magazines, their greatest form of marketing has been the utilization of recipes. These custom-formulated recipes incorporate their products, and individuals like them so much they have even developed their own cookbook.

The Cumberland Culinary Center™ also opened up the group to yet another opportunity. Their management of the facility meant they had an active role with every company who utilized the kitchen. Over time, they began to pick up on the positive actions and activities of companies which were succeeding. Conversely, they saw the mistakes many individuals made as they were trying to live out the dream of bringing their own products to market.

With the knowledge they had gathered, they began offering consulting services to assist start-ups with the rules, regulations and best practices to be successful. Sue provides the nutritional information and formulation profiling. Tom assists companies with product and packaging design.

Sue and Gary will literally walk individuals through the entire process of going from a home cooking hobbyist to a business that sells to consumers at retail.

Their own business has continued to thrive as well. They have expanded into Whole Foods® and also gotten into Kroger® in addition to specialty and gourmet stores. Their online business is solid as well.

A typical day for Sue and Gary begins around 4:00 a.m. They work on the business side of their food business filling out paperwork and fulfilling web orders.

The Cumberland Culinary Center™ operates up to six days-a-week. When it is running, Gary and Sue arrive there around 7:00 a.m. for pre-operations and sanitizing. When the client arrives, they either stay to oversee production for new users or are simply on call for experienced clients. Should anything go wrong with any of the machinery, Gary must get it fixed so the client can continue completing their product run.

It's pretty safe to say that Sue, Gary and Tom shed the idea of working for someone else when they left the telecommunications industry. They are now about as entrepreneurial as you can get!

By the way, if you need a Japanese Maple, Gary specializes in them and has a side gig selling those. Yet another business for the team of Sue Sykes, Gary Dummer and Tom Ellison!

Tennessee Gourmet Photo Album

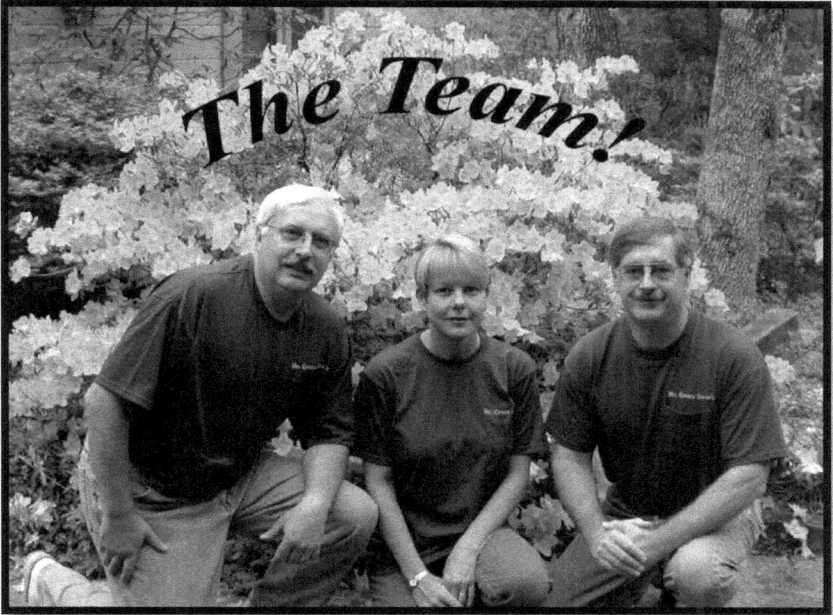

Gary Dummer, Sue Sykes and Tom Ellison

The Cumberland Culinary Center™

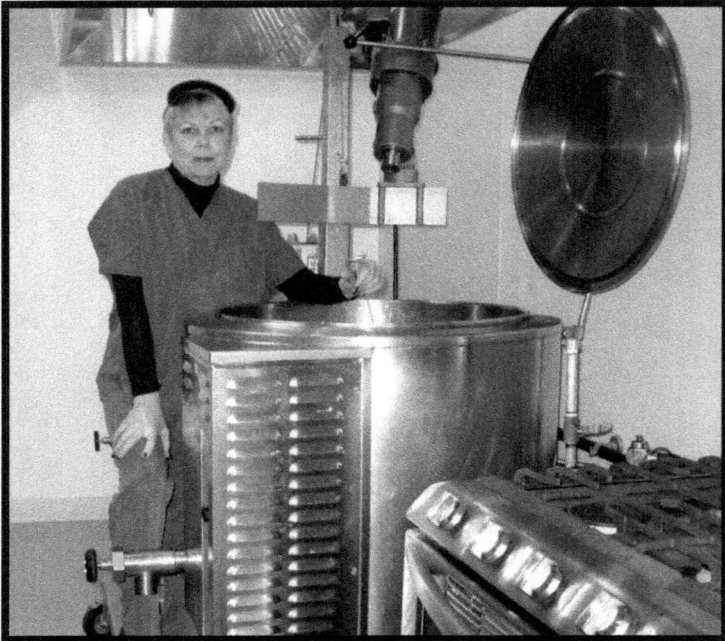

Sue cooking at the Cumberland Culinary Center™

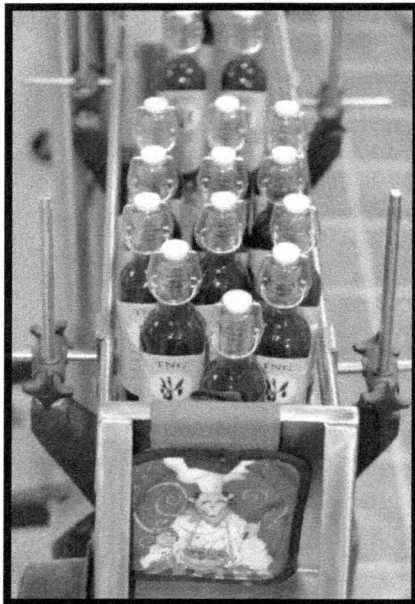

Product rolling off of the line

Tennessee Gourmet's pepper jelly includes ghost peppers, one of the hottest peppers in the world

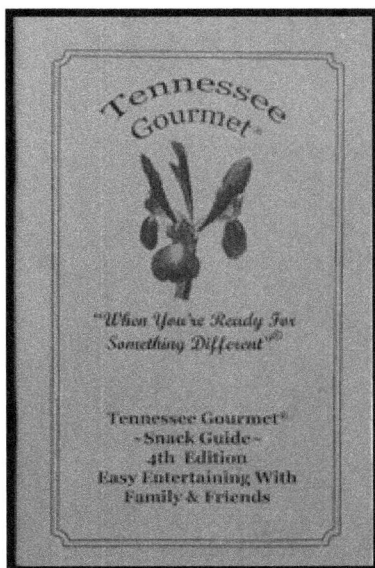

Tennessee Gourmet's Snack Guide features recipes incorporating its products

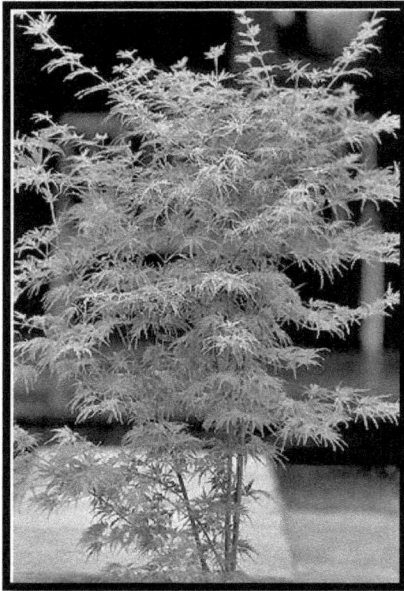

One of Gary's Japanese Maples

Tennessee Gourmet's product lineup

Chapter 9: Pretzels
Gus' Pretzels

1820 Arsenal
St. Louis, MO 63118
(314) 664 - 4010

guspretzels.com

Established
1920

Leadership
Gus & Suzanne Koebbe, Owners

Products
Soft baked pretzels and dips

As iconic in St. Louis as large steel arches, birds on bats, foam topped beverages and Clydesdales…

Any true St. Louisan knows a great freshly baked pretzel. They are lucky enough to live in a city where the artistry of making and baking fresh pretzels is still appreciated. You see, they live where Gus' Pretzel has been rolling along since 1920. It's worth noting that the company is conveniently located right in the shadow of another St. Louis institution: Anheuser-Busch®. (After all, is there a more perfect pairing than a beer and a pretzel?)

For the true St. Louisan, with their pretzel palette refined by years of Gus' enjoyment, the large microwaveable megabrand offerings taste like compacted sawdust. No worries: third-generation owner Gus' Koebbe and wife Suzanne have brought Gus' into the homes of the community with their own line of home-baked pretzels and an accompanying line of dipping sauces.

The business started in 1920. Well, at least 1920. Gus and Suzanne know the business existed before then, but there isn't a written history of exactly when the business started. They have confirmed 1920 from family members, so it has become the official year they list as the beginning of the business. It began when Gus' grandfather, a welder by trade, got hurt on the job and needed to do something different. He started a pretzel business.

He would bake pretzels which would be sold wholesale to street vendors who would sell them at busy intersections all over St. Louis. At the end of the day, he would take any remaining pretzels and go out and sell them himself.

The business carried on as a one-man operation until Gus Sr. (current owner Gus Jr.'s father) began working in the business. The business continued to grow with Gus' father at the helm, but mostly he kept it to the core of being primarily a wholesale business supplying vendors to sell their product retail.

In his first day of college at Southeast Missouri State, Gus Jr. met his future wife. He was meeting some friends to head to a beer blowout when he ran into an acquaintance who introduced Gus to his girlfriend, Suzanne, who was heading into the library to do some studying (it seems Gus and Suzanne had very different ideas of what college was all about).

Gus and Suzanne maintained a friendship over the course of the next several years. Even after her relationship with her boyfriend ended, she had stayed in the group of friends Gus also ran with. By their junior year they had officially started dating. Ultimately, the two fell in love and would get married and move to St. Louis (Suzanne had been from Ste. Genevieve, Missouri, a historic town about an hour south of St. Louis). The plan was for them to take over the pretzel business which was something Suzanne was very comfortable being involved in as her father had run his own family business back in Ste. Genevieve.

This ended up being the perfect plan for all involved because Gus' Pretzels had been back to a one-man operation while Gus Jr. was away at college and Gus Sr. was ready to retire. In 1980, Gus and Suzanne bought out Gus Sr. and officially began running the business.

This started a 30+ year run of growth where Gus and Suzanne would radically expand the business, while steadfastly maintaining the integrity and quality of their product through careful planning each step of the way. Their first step to expanding the business beyond what they were doing was through a personal friendship Gus had. When a buddy took over ownership of a small independent grocer from his father, he asked Gus about carrying Gus' Pretzels in his store.

Selling frozen dough was something his father and grandfather had tried before him, but it had not worked. Despite the warnings of past bad experiences, Gus felt he had little to lose by trying to sell unbaked pretzels at retail since he was doing this with a friend. They put his pretzels in the store, and they quickly began selling. So much so that the large, multi-store chains quickly began to take notice.

When a buyer at one of the larger chains in St. Louis called him about carrying Gus' in their stores, Gus informed him he really didn't have the infrastructure to deliver to their stores. He didn't have a delivery truck, nor did he have the extra staff to drop them at the individual locations. All of his time was accounted for running the shop and making the product for his customers, and the grocery store of his friend. (It should be noted he also picked up a couple of other stores from that relationship as well. Other stores affiliated with the warehouse servicing his friend's store convinced Gus to sell them pretzels as well.)

Delivering the pretzels was the only sticking point? No problem.

The buyer worked out a deal with Gus. He would personally pick up the pretzels and deliver them to two of his stores. As they sold and Gus had income coming in to the point where he could get a delivery truck and staff, Gus could then deliver them to the rest of their stores in St. Louis. The only stipulation was he couldn't start selling to any of the other three major chains in St. Louis until he got to the point where he could service all of their stores.

Deal!

Guess what? Once Gus' was introduced in the first of the four large chains in St. Louis, the rest wanted his products in their stores as well. He had the first of the chains covered, but he didn't have the freezer space to store the wholesale products for distribution to the other stores. Again, no problem. The second of the four large chains offered their freezer space to him if he would sell to their stores.

Soon, Gus was in all four chains and other smaller independents in St. Louis. When the microwave pretzel became the standard, Gus' added a line of microwave pretzels to his business mix as well. He already had the distribution system in place so adding a new product was easy for him.

Over time, the microwave pretzels became so popular, the frozen dough was discontinued everywhere other than one small retailer and Gus' own store which is attached to his pretzel factory.

The next big change for the company came in 1998. Coming to Gus' meant parking on the street and walking down a very narrow alley and walking directly into the kitchen where an employee would have to stop baking to sell customers pretzels. Gus decided to open up his own parking lot and a store front which was accessible directly from the parking lot and the street. He, Suzanne and Gus' brother Dave redesigned the building incorporating a glass enclosed kitchen where customers could watch pretzels being made as they waited. They also added a complete line of items which included pretzel covered brats, salsiccias (an Italian sausage) and hot dogs. These sandwich offerings were something they had perfected when they had tried to branch out to a storefront in a local mall years ago. It didn't work out there but was the perfect offering for their newly revamped building.

Their walk-up business increased threefold on the first day and has maintained those solid numbers ever since. Gus and Suzanne have managed to maintain a loyal customer following by continuing with the ideals of Gus' grandfather and father: make a quality product at a quality price and customers will keep coming back.

The final addition to Gus' Pretzels product line came from a chance encounter Suzanne had. When she was visiting home in Ste. Genevieve, one of the many shops there had their own branded mustard. She thought it would be a great idea to have something similar for Gus'. The shop owner shared their manufacturer with Suzanne, and she was able to begin working with them to start a line of mustard and dipping sauces for Gus'.

In addition to several mustards they only carry at their store, Gus' has the following dips available at local grocers in St. Louis: Red Raspberry Pretzel Dip, Monterey Jack Con Queso, Pub Beer Mustard Dip and a Honey Mustard Dip. These have been a welcome addition to the mix for Gus' and help advertise his core business with each sale of them at retail.

The future looks very bright for this 94 year old business. The next generation of Koebbes has entered the business. Gus III has worked at the business for the last 7 years. Daughter Allison works outside of the business in human resources but is able to offer plenty of help and direction for Gus' and its 18 employees with her experience in that field.

At 58, Gus plans on continuing to work for several years. He notes that he and Suzanne had the difficulty of taking over the business all by themselves when they first started. Gus and Suzanne plan to stick around to ease the transition of taking over the business for their children.

Gus happily notes that the plan moving forward is up in the air. He states he was not laying out an action plan each year, he was able to roll with opportunities as they came to him. He foresees plenty of opportunities to be available for Gus III as he takes over the helm.

He could easily see his children expanding the retail sale of their products beyond St. Louis. They could also look at launching internet sales. It's not uncommon for Gus' to field 10 – 15 calls in a week asking them to ship pretzels somewhere mail order. The typically call involves someone who has moved from St. Louis and is just looking for a taste of home with a Gus' pretzel. They aren't set-up to do this so they have to politely decline these requests.

Then again, Gus III and Allison just might keep rolling along and selling pretzels out of their flagship store down the street from Anheuser-Busch®. After all, it's been a pretty solid business plan for almost 100 years already!

Gus' Pretzels Photo Album

Gus and Suzanne Koebbe

Gus' Pretzel Shop

The entrance to the shop

Gus' father served in WWII before working in the family pretzel business

Gus' Pretzels are a popular item to bring to parties, like this one for Gus' mom's 94th birthday

Gus packaging pretzels

Three generations of "Gus" pretzel makers

Gus frozen pretzel packaging

Gus' Pretzels product lineup

Chapter 10: Handmade Spices
Rockerbox Garlic

Millbrook, NY
(631) 794 - 9418

rockerboxgarlic.com
rockerboxgarlic@gmail.com

Established
2012

Leadership
Rae Rotindo, Owner

Products
Handmade spices including: garlic powder, garlic flakes, red and onion yellow powder, shallot powder, spice blends and other garlic products

No vampires were harmed in the writing of this chapter...

A simple health screening for Rockerbox Garlic owner Rae Rotindo would likely tell you everything you need to know about her passion for her business. You see, unlike the general population, somewhere in her report, tucked in the usual measures of triglycerides, HDL, LDL and the rest of the unidentifiable measurements in these screenings, would be something unique: garlic.

That's right, clearly garlic courses through her veins!

Rae's great-grandfather moved from Sicily to New York where he became a garlic farmer. She was born in Houston, Texas, but her family moved back to their native New York roots of Ossining, New York, in the Hudson Valley when she was a young child.

Living in New York meant she became closer to her grandparents. Her grandfather was now carrying on the tradition of garlic farming his father had started. A farmer, he grew grapes, tomatoes and other produce but garlic was his passion. She recalls fondly the braids of garlic hanging throughout the rafters as he cured them.

While they lived about six hours away, when they did visit, Rae would enjoy helping him in selling his garlic. Whether it was at his roadside stand or at a farmers' market, it was always a lot of fun for her. During the down times he would keep her interest by challenging her or her cousins to eat a whole clove of garlic.

At the farmers' market they would generate interest in their product by grilling garlic cloves to the point of them being a warm, flavorful paste which they would serve to potential customers on crackers.

Despite this passion for the family business, initially it didn't look like her career path would lead back to garlic. Always an excellent student, she sought a career in science. After graduating with a degree in Astrophysics and Environmental Sciences from Stony Brook University in Long Island, she got a job in the field of environmental science in New York City.

While the work was rewarding, the environment and structure of the organization made for a terrible work experience. Her personal life was going well (she had gotten married) but the negative situation of her job began to take a toll on her.

She began to look for diversions in her personal life which could take her out of the stress she was experiencing on the job. She found refuge in cooking. While experimenting with a dehydrator she had purchased for her husband to make beef jerky, she discovered she could dry cloves of garlic and in turn utilize them to make garlic powder or flakes which was absolutely nothing like the processed, filler-fueled product she found labeled "garlic powder" at the grocery store. This tasted like the garlic she and her grandfather had harvested fresh on the family farm for so many summers in her youth.

Friends and family loved what she was doing. Of course, they can be a slightly tainted test audience, so she decided to seek out the opinions of others. She became involved in a few "food swap" clubs. These are organizations where individuals bring homegrown or homemade foods to trade.

The feedback she got from the individuals in these groups was overwhelmingly strong; she needed to look to sell her product commercially. She began to hear from several people that she needed to approach Brooklyn Kitchen™, a gourmet food store which would be a perfect fit for her product.

On a whim she decided to speak to the buyers of Brooklyn Kitchen™ to see if they might be interested in her garlic powder. After sampling her product, they were ready to order. Of course, she was just a hobbyist seeking to judge the viability of bringing her homemade product to market. At that point, she didn't even have a logo or label for her garlic powder!

With confirmed interest and a job that continued to get worse, she decided to take a really big chance. She quit her job. At this point she still wasn't 100% committed to pursuing her own business just yet. She decided to continue to actively seek a new job while also working hard on getting her spice company up-and-running.

Her plan of action was to blanket New York gourmet shops with samples of her product. Her goal: 100 stores. She got to work on the labor intensive process of creating 100 jars of her Rockerbox Garlic Powder. She then hustled around the city, shaking hands and delivering those 100 samples.

Everybody loves a happy ending, especially when it's the "little guy" succeeding. Life isn't always that easy, though. After pouring her heart-and-soul into blanketing New York's gourmet food scene, she got... crickets. Her phone didn't ring. Orders weren't pouring in.

Finally, one store called her and placed an order. For many, a 1% response might very well mean the end of the dream. For the entrepreneur, 1% means that you've got interest. It represented a small flame burning which needed to be stoked.

That affirmation was exactly what Rae needed. The job search was over. Just like her family for generations before her, she was in the garlic business!

The small margin of success in her sample distribution did show her she would need to seek a different route for her company rather than just taking it directly to stores. She began cultivating customers one at a time via different means. She built a web site. This featured the story of her company, recipes and offered the ability for customers to order her products. She started actively participating in farmers' markets and festivals and maintaining an active Facebook® page.

Slowly, and organically, her business began to grow. She started to garner a loyal following of her product. The interest of individuals who tried her product also led to new opportunities in retail so her wholesale business began to grow as well. Today, her family is no longer involved in farming garlic, at least not commercially. Her grandfather had passed away while she was in college, and the family farm was sold. Several members of the family continue to farm garlic as a hobby from the original strands her grandfather and great-grandfather had grown.

Her distribution continues to grow. She now sells her product in stores in California, Florida, Connecticut and New Hampshire in addition to the areas in New York surrounding her home-base of Millbrook.

While she continues to produce all of her products herself at this point, she is getting close to needing to hire some help. This was something that would have been very difficult to envision just a short time ago. She can now look back on her lowest moment… no job and a response rate of 1% to her initial foray into the business and look back fondly at the lessons learned.

She states, "For me grit is one of the key words used to describe what you need to be successful as an entrepreneur. It's the drive to keep going forward for success even when everything is indicating you should quit. Trust me, through all of this, I have needed a lot of grit."

The name "Rockerbox" comes from a mining term for a tool which sifts through dirt to find gold. Rae utilized it after taking five labor intensive days to create and jar her first batch. Her husband Michael, conveying how impressed he was with her efforts, told her that each jar was just like gold.

Knowing that garlic, like gold, comes from the earth and involved sifting away dirt, it seemed like a natural pairing to her so she ran with the name Rockerbox.

Of course the real gold in the equation for Rockerbox may very well be Rae Rotindo herself. After all, a great product is always a good first start for a profitable business, but by no means guarantees success. It takes the vision, drive, and yes, plenty of grit. It's what Rae brings to the table and that is what is going to make Rockerbox a success.

Rockerbox Garlic Photo Album

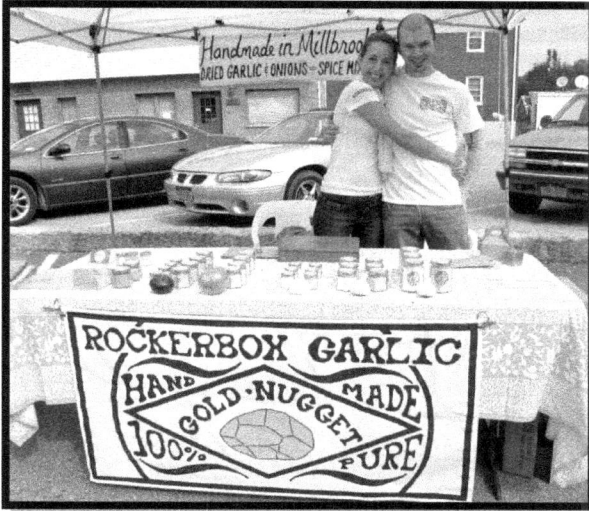

Rae Rotindo and her husband Michael at a farmers' market

Rae's grandfather and great-grandfather working on the farm

Rae's mother is an artist and she's picked up a few skills she uses to create the signs she uses at her farmers' markets

Even her business cards are reflective of her artistic skills

Rae's products in Brooklyn Kitchen™ (her first store)

Garlic spread, like the roasted garlic paste she used to sample at farmers' markets with her grandfather is another product line

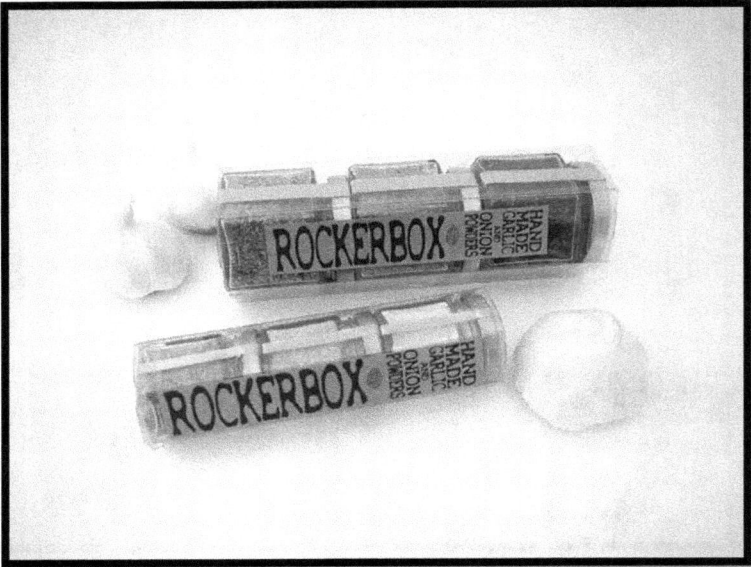

Gift packs

Rockerbox product lineup

Chapter 11: Honey
Catskill Provisions, Inc.

244 Delaware Lake Road
Long Eddy, NY 12760
(845) 418 - 6482

catskillprovisions.com
info@catskillprovisions.com

Established
2010

Leadership
Claire Marin, Co-Founder & Beekeeper
Cathy Leidersdorff, Co-Founder

Products
Wildflower honeys, honeycomb, maple syrup, barbecue sauces, marinades, pancake mixes, all-natural ketchup, maple sugar, truffles and honey whiskey

Über committed to the concept of being produced locally…

Claire Marin is so committed to a closed-loop system on making her locally-produced product, there is a rumor she asks vendors what they had for breakfast. She wants to ensure they ate locally produced foods to start their day so they are fueled to work on anything associated with her goods by "made in New York" products only.

Why not?

She produces all of her products in New York, using locally sourced ingredients. Everything is packaged and labeled in New York. Most of the bottles she packages her products in are made locally. She even checks to see where the ink is produced on the labels printed for her items. Yes, that is a commitment to "produced locally and made in New York."

Despite this staunch commitment to The Empire State, she didn't always live there. Claire, whose mother was from Spain and father from France, grew up in Madrid. Her father had a government job, and he was transferred to São Paulo, Brazil, when she was 10 years old.

They lived in Brazil until she was 14 when the family moved again. This time they relocated to New York where Claire truly felt at home. This, despite the fact it meant she was learning her fourth language (Spanish, French, Portuguese and English) at a time when many individuals struggle with feelings of awkwardness and seek acceptance of their peers. (She continues to be able to speak all four languages today.)

This would also begin the love of New York she would carry over to her business years later.

Before starting Catskill Provisions, she had a career in magazine publishing which started out in advertising sales. Ultimately she would work her way to the VP, Publisher level for such magazines as **Woman's Day**, **Town & Country** and **Elle Décor.**

Around 2003, she started beekeeping as a hobby. She had started to become disillusioned with the publishing industry as it struggled to remain relevant in a world segmented by mobile feeds, 24-hour access to news and the constant contact of Twitter® and other social media.

Not only did working with the bees help Claire keep her sanity, it also gave her a fun hobby she could share with friends. She began bottling the honey and giving it to friends as gifts. They would rave about how good it was and encourage her to try selling it.

A bee hive is a living community with a complex hierarchy which survives by all members committing to the betterment of the group as a whole. Every bee has a role, and as long as they each work diligently in their specific duty, the hive not only survives, it thrives.

By 2009, Claire found her career to be a little "unbee-like" as she puts it. Simply put, she was ready to make a change in her life.

The good news for her, she was in the envious position of being able to leave her job and settle onto her 32-acre farm in the Catskill Mountains. There, she would be able to pursue her dream to produce the most wonderful honey and maple syrup (another local favorite) available anywhere.

With what would become her signature look, she found a hex jar, black cap and orange label with a logo designed via a contest on crowdSPRING® (*crowdspring.com*). The end result was a clean, inviting look which had a great deal of shelf appeal.

For her honey business, she would only offer wildflower honey and would stick to only the highest quality batches to jar. Once she started jarring her product, Claire began distribution on her own getting the product into stores by calling around and delivering samples. She tried a distributor but found little return on her investment so she decided to continue handling these duties on her own.

Her second product was also going to assist Claire in her goal of bringing revenue and jobs to the area. She had found locally produced maple syrup to be the some of the finest quality to come out of the U.S. Despite the abundance of "friends, family and neighbors" producers, she believes Catskills maple syrup was underrepresented in the marketplace.

She evaluated two business models to start her maple syrup business. She could buy the tap and buckets and other equipment needed to produce maple syrup or she could work with local maple syrup farmers and buy their excess.

She didn't see how ramping up her own maple syrup business would be productive or help her bring money to her hometown. In fact, it might have the opposite effect. She would find herself in direct competition with those she really wanted to help.

She quickly decided the way to go would be to pursue developing strategic partnerships with those already producing maple syrup in the area.

Lucky for her, one of her neighbors was a big producer of maple syrup, and he was happy to pursue a wholesale relationship with her. She formulated a blend of syrup grades which would become the product she sold. At the same time, she also worked out similar deals with other local hobbyist maple syrup producers in addition to her neighbor. Her handshake deal to them included the fact they were free to sell their own branded product in the local stores in town as they always had. She agreed to sell her Catskill Provisions in the markets outside of their immediate hometown of Long Eddy, New York, so she wouldn't be invading their turf.

With two product lines Claire was officially on a roll. She began experimenting with recipes, both on her own as well as with local chefs to add more products to the fold. Soon, she also had a pancake mix, all-natural ketchup, barbecue sauces and line of marinades. She also developed a line of honey truffles which are representative of the ultimate "Made in New York" decadence.

Her finest achievement may be her latest addition to Catskill Provisions' portfolio: New York Honey, her honey-flavored whiskey.

That's right, she's joined the likes of such great American whiskey makers as Jack Daniels, Jim Beam and Booker Noe. Initially, she had pursued the idea of distilling her whiskey herself, but it would have required a tremendous investment of both capital and time.

Once again, partnering locally seemed a much better option. She worked with nearby Finger Lakes Distillery® to formulate a recipe using her honey. They do the distilling, and she does the distributing. Yep, she managed to find another way to fund her own personal "support local" campaign.

Claire not only takes pride into investing into the local economy, but by the fact she has products which are not only good, but better for you than those being offered by the bigger brands. She has mothers writing to her about her all-natural ketchup. They say it is the favorite of their children which is incredibly rewarding for her knowing she has introduced kids to a healthier option of one of their favorite condiments since hers doesn't contain high fructose corn syrup typically found in the offerings from the megabrands.

She also believes with her New York Honey whiskey she has completed the line expansions for Catskill Provisions. She has developed a complete line of products complementing the raw ingredients available to be sourced locally.

She envisions Catskill Provisions continuing to grow and expand but staying a regional brand. If she decides she wants to seek further adventures in the food industry, she would choose a different area of the country and begin a similar strategy of building a portfolio of products representative of that area.

The growth for the company now should be coming from her whiskey. The flavored whiskey market is a growing segment, and hers has the unique appeal of being a locally sourced artisan product using real honey and not artificial flavors. Claire is planning to spend the bulk of her time and efforts establishing and growing her brand over the next several years. Ideally, this will lead to a whole new audience of whiskey drinkers discovering the rest of her Catskill Provisions catalog.

It's probably safe to say the big liquor companies haven't yet started worrying about Claire Marin and her personal quest to get everyone to buy New York products. Those fine companies from Tennessee and Kentucky shouldn't overlook her for long, though. She's on a mission and won't be denied.

Don't believe it?

Just ask her label printer. He just took a phone call where he had to promise he actually ate a locally sourced breakfast this morning!

Catskill Provisions Photo Album

Claire Marin

The employees of Catskill Provisions

Claire on the radio promoting her company

Working with the bees

That's more than a cord!

Truffles… yum!

Catskill Provisions' news product: Honey Flavored Whiskey

Catskill Provisions product lineup

Chapter 12: Hot Sauce & Specialty Foods
Dave's Gourmet, Inc.

2000 McKinnon Avenue
Building 428 #5
San Francisco, CA 94124
(415) 401 - 9100

davesgourmet.com.com
info@davesgourmet.com

Established
1993

Leadership
Dave Hirschkop, Founder, President & Spice Meister

Products
A complete line of hot sauces, including their flagship Dave's Gourmet Insanity Sauce along with pasta sauces, snacks, drink mixes, savory sauces and other specialty food items

"What makes a chili hot in the first place?"...

Take a gregarious personality; add an incredible drive and pursuit of excellence, along with a commitment to helping others and you've got Dave Hirschkop. These traits, which he would parlay into a company that would take the hot sauce category by storm, were readily apparent even before Dave's Gourmet was created.

Dave grew up in Alexandria, Virginia. In high school he started a non-profit to raise awareness and money to fight hunger in Africa. His plans for college were going to take him in a different direction. After perhaps watching a few too many James Bond™ movies, he decided he wanted to be an international spy. He went with a curriculum focusing on Russian studies. As Communism crumbled, so did Dave's desire to be a spy, so he began to look for his next move.

Even with the change in heart about his major, he continued to support charitable works. One summer, he joined a group of individuals (mostly college students) who biked across the United States to raise money for hunger in the U.S. and Africa. Each person coordinated two cities along the way where they would work with the local media, participate in fundraising or sometimes simply enjoy sightseeing on their adventure. That summer, Dave biked over 3,000 miles, raised a lot of money for charity and slept on a lot of gym floors.

After graduation from Boston University, Dave moved to California to be with a woman he had met while studying in London during his second to last semester at B.U. When that relationship ended, he moved back home on the East Coast, landing in College Park, Maryland, home of the University of Maryland.

It was in College Park where Dave opened a restaurant. His menu was a combination of wraps and creative burritos. Dave began experimenting with creating his own sauces for his burritos and wraps. He also found he could tame some of the late night rowdy students if he made the sauces progressively hotter.

He couldn't seem to find the ceiling for hot sauce. The hotter he would make it, the hotter people would continue to challenge him to go. The machismo-fueled games of attempting to try the hottest hot sauce he offered was great marketing for a restaurant in a college town.

At the time (early 90s), making a sauce hotter meant either getting hotter peppers, or increasing the amount of peppers versus other ingredients (or both for really hot sauces). Since Dave was looking to make the hottest sauce possible, he asked himself, "What makes a hot sauce hot?" If he could figure out the answer to this question, he could isolate that component and then really make a hot sauce.

With the passion of an international spy, he began researching the science of peppers (not as easy to do pre-internet as it would be today with a simple search). He was pleased to find out not only was his work done for him (capsaicin is the active component to chili peppers), it had already been isolated out. Capsaicin could be found in such products as pepper spray or pain reliever creams like Bengay™.

Dave's Insanity Sauce, as he called it, was an instant hit at the restaurant. It did so well, and created such a buzz, on a whim, Dave decided to package it and take it to the Fiery Foods Show™ in Albuquerque, New Mexico. He created a real stir by debuting the product there while wearing a straightjacket. He received national media coverage with the imagery of him in the straightjacket, hawking an "Insanity Sauce" which ended up being so hot it got banned from the show.

Banned from a show with "Fiery Foods" in its name?

Now that's an accomplishment.

With the national coverage of Dave's Insanity Sauce, and the fact it had totally created a new category of sauces (it was 6 to 8 times hotter than anything else on the market), Dave began getting phone calls for orders. Prior to this happening, he didn't even know there was such a thing as a hot sauce shop. He did now, and they were calling him wanting his Insanity Sauce.

With the long hours, low margins and the competitive nature of the restaurant business, Dave thought this was the perfect time to exit the industry. He sold his restaurant and secured a job as a mortgage broker back in California. The plan was for him to move back there and work full-time as a mortgage broker, or something else if he ended up not liking it. He was going to keep doing Dave's Insanity as a side business. It was to be a hobby he could dedicate his time to on the weekends to generate some extra income.

After about a year of doing this, and another appearance at the Fiery Foods Show™, this time with his psychiatric nurse, Dave was ready to dedicate himself full-time to his hot sauce business. The media had once again given him an incredible amount of coverage as the "banned sauce" was allowed to return based on popular demand from hot sauce aficionados.

Starting out part-time was great because it allowed Dave to get his business in order without having to taking profits out of it. With his full-time attention he was able to do much more. One of his first accomplishments was he was to expand his product line to go beyond just hot sauce. It made sense to do this when you consider a few drops of his flagship Insanity Sauce could heat up an entire pot of chili. You aren't going to get many turns on a product where a single bottle is dishing out a drop at time.

Clearly Dave has an eye for marketing. He has been able to parlay a hot sauce into appearances on Good Morning America™, the Today Show™, Food Network™ Shows, every major newspaper and even his all-time favorite, *GQ Magazine*™ (he proudly claims to be the least attractive model to ever appear in *GQ*™). His greatest piece of marketing wasn't an interview or TV appearance, though. It was his approach to his brand.

Realizing his early customers were hot sauce specialty stores and gift shops, he began taking an approach used in the wine and distilled spirits industry by offering a limited edition reserve of Dave's Insanity Sauce. These special formulations would be uniquely packaged, offered in small production runs and would be individually numbered and signed by Dave. This took him beyond simply a hot sauce company. It truly gave him a brand. It also meant his special "Reserve" offerings were the perfect anchor to a display of his items in the stores.

This was huge for Dave because as he expanded the line, the Reserve would be the centerpiece to all of his other products. This kept "the family" together. He didn't have any "orphans" (for instance, his salsa wasn't stocked away from the rest of his products where it might be lost on a top shelf over larger more well-known competitors in that particular category). Everything was kept together so customers could shop a Dave's Gourmet section. (It should be noted that the Special Reserve editions would become coveted collector's items with the hot sauce crowd and continue to demand high prices on the secondary market.)

The new approach to hot sauce (the hottest sauces possible and special limited edition products), the media coverage, the brand extensions through new product offerings and the presence of a grouped family of products meant Dave's Gourmet sat atop the specialty hot sauce category as the industry leader. Twenty years in, it's a spot Dave still occupies today. Of course, specialty hot sauce is just a blip on the radar compared to the traditional hot sauce category you find in grocery stores. Dave has taken the next step in the evolution of his company by entering this domain as well.

The future of his company is going to be continuing to do what he has done to get him here: innovation. He wants to continue to add product lines which will help him grow his brand. His pasta sauce line has really been growing recently, and he's made some real progress on expanding distribution. Once again, he took a different approach over what he was finding on shelves.

He noticed there were two types of pasta sauces on the shelves: megabrands (low quality offerings with huge marketing budgets) and family recipes. Dave didn't have a family recipe he could offer to a pasta sauce, but he did have a different idea.

What about if he took a "chef's approach" to making a sauce?

After all, he was based in California. It was home to some of the finest ingredients which serve as the base of any good sauce (heirloom tomatoes and garlic). He worked with top chefs to help him create sauces using those locally sourced ingredients, and he came up with a sauce he believed was superior to anything he could find on the market. His approach has worked because it is his most rapidly growing product and certainly offers greater turns over his flagship Dave's Insanity Sauce.

Dave Hirschkop plans on continuing to grow Dave's Gourmet for a long time to come. Unless we enter another Cold War era with Russia. If that happens, Dave will undoubtedly be checking with the CIA to see if they need an international spy with a background in Russian studies and hot sauce.

Dave's Gourmet, Inc. Photo Album

Dave Hirschkop

Dave's flagship Insanity Sauce

The ghost pepper is the "it" pepper today when it comes to heat. Dave features it in both a hot sauce…

…and a salsa

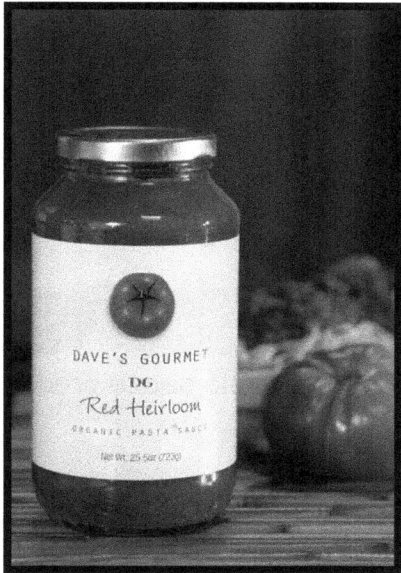

Dave sees opportunities in his pasta sauce line

Meet the Scorpion Pepper

Dave's Gourmet pasta sauce product lineup

Dave's Gourmet Insanity Sauces product lineup

Chapter 12: Ice Cream
Three Twins Ice Cream

419 1st Street
Petaluma, CA 94952
(707) 763 – TWIN (8946)

threetwinsicecream.com
customersservice@threetwinsicecream.com

Established
2005

Leadership
Neal Gottlieb, Founder and Owner

Products
Certified organic premium ice cream

Three Twins Ice Cream: Fulfilling the "inner do-gooder" of Neal Gottlieb and the sweet tooth of the rest of us…

Upon graduation from Cornell University, Neal Gottlieb was not an "ice cream guy." At that point he was a "finance guy," working in a management training program for Gap, Inc®.

The company was solid, and the work was exactly what Neal had gone to school for, but there was simply something missing. He found himself longing for a position where he was personally doing something more for the greater good and society in general. While he searched for those answers within himself, he continued working for Gap®.

When the tragedy of September 11 occurred, his vision of what he should be doing with his life became a little more clear, and he could no longer work a corporate job. He gave up a fast-track, and safe, career path for something much less assured, but infinity more fulfilling: the Peace Corp.

He signed up for a 27 month tour of duty where he would be working in Morocco. This was the Peace Corp's only presence in an Arab country during the War in Afghanistan. His service time was cut short when tensions mounted, and the Peace Corp volunteers were evacuated.

Upon his return to the United States, Neal considered going back to school for a business degree. As he looked deeper into this plan, he felt a general business degree would lead to the same dissatisfaction he had incurred when he was pursuing his finance career.

He knew the only way he would truly be happy was to balance business with the "inner do-gooder" in him. He began searching for ideas for his own business when he came up with ice cream.

While ice cream with a social conscious had been done before, nobody had ever built an ice cream brand (on any sort of scale) based upon the combination of an organic product without artificial colors, flavors, or stabilizers, featuring a corporate philosophy and financial structure based on being socially conscious.

The idea of ice cream, as a product, made sense for Neal for many reasons:

- ***There was room for improvement*** – Sure, there were numerous players on a local, national and even international scale for ice cream. Still, he had ideas which would take him beyond what any of these players had ever come up with. Even with the popularity of ice cream, there was simply still room to improve what was being done.

- ***Room for error*** – Although Neal didn't have a background in ice cream (make that literally no ice cream experience), he felt working in ice cream was a forgiving medium. He was going to be experimenting with flavors and ingredients to come up with his own unique offerings, but he could still serve up his experiments as he went along because when you are working in ice cream, even your worst effort can be pretty darn good!

- ***Store versus Home Experience*** – Because Neal was offering a product which he hoped to build into a national brand, he thought the best way would be to offer his product on-site first, then build his brand by offering it retail. He believes no product, other than ice cream is conducive to this approach. He felt like the coffee or pizza you have in a store is different than the "take home" versions of it. Ice cream is different though. The exact same product and experience in a store can be recreated in the home because the product itself is exactly the same.

- ***Premium Segment*** – Finally, Neal believed ice cream is also different than many segments in the grocery store in that consumers have already proven they can differentiate between a regular and premium version of the product. Consumers understand not all ice creams are the same, and there is a rather large segment of consumers looking for a premium product when it comes to ice cream, and they are willing to pay more for a product which exceeds lesser competitors in terms of quality.

During his time working, Neal had managed to save $70,000 which he would use to start the business. His seed money, along with a loan of $25,000 from his parents, would be what he needed to get his business going. Thinking the name "Neal's Ice Cream" wasn't enough to bank a brand on, he decided to take a name for the company from his personal life: Three Twins. It came from the fact he was living with his twin brother Carl and his fiancée Liz, who also happened to be a twin. They had been calling their home "Three Twins," and it seemed to be a catchy name to call Neal's new brand.

Neal took a two-day commercial ice cream class to prepare himself for working with ice cream. He was able to secure a lease for a storefront in San Raphael, but it would require some major renovations. After finally working through a major revamp for the store, Neal opened for business. Not being able to afford help, he was the only employee for the company.

Neal would make ice cream in the morning. He would open the shop during the day and scoop everything he had made in the morning. In the evening he would clean-up and take care of accounting and paperwork.

While he always had the goal of expanding the company, it took time. As his business began to grow profits were utilized to hire employees to assist him. About a year-and-a-half into business, he began hand-packing and labeling pints to sell at stores.

Around the same time, everything else was beginning to fall in place for Neal with the business as well. Three Twins received its "Certified Organic" designation through the California Certified Organic Farms™ organization. Additionally, Three Twins became a 1% for the Planet™ member.

1% for the Planet™ is an organization which connects companies willing to donate 1% of their sales "off of the top" (regardless of profitability) to charitable organizations benefitting the planet. Three Twins has designated a variety of non-profits benefitting land conservation.

Over time, Neal's whole business grew to the point where he could no longer manage producing and packaging ice cream in his store. In 2008 he opened a state-of-the-art factory which helped him increase production from a few hundred hand-packed pints a day in his store to 12,000 pints a day.

At this point he was no longer just a single store operation. He had four scoop shops, a stand at the Berkley Farmers' market, food service agreements making his product available at restaurants and cafés, licensing agreements for other scoop shops to offer his ice cream, and nationwide distribution through grocers and other retailers.

The certified organic community can be leery of large scale growth like Neal has experienced with Three Twins. Often when the economies of scale go up, companies begin to look to cut corners to lower cost on their larger production runs. There is no need to worry about Three Twins turning its back on its commitment to stay certified organic. Neal realizes the importance of the designation, and what it means to his company.

In fact, the growth has been great for his creativity in the certified organic realm. As a small company, he struggled with securing partners for ingredients. As he has built his company up, with the amount of buying power he now has, he has been able to find vendors willing to become certified organic for their ingredients. It was strategic partnerships with companies willing to become certified organic to work with Three Twins which allowed Neal to offer the first salted caramel and chocolate peanut butter cup certified organic ice creams.

Today, the business is exactly as Neal had envisioned it when he started. In addition to the 1% for the Planet™ partnership, in 2011, Three Twins also started its own land conservation program entitled Ice Cream for Acres. Through strategic partnerships with charitable organizations, Three Twins is able to offer land conservation donations tied to each unit of ice cream they sell. For instance, a pint of ice cream saves six square feet of land. An ice cream sandwich secures two square feet. Through their website they literally track the square footage of land preserved and the numbers are staggering to see, and fun to watch as they go up with each purchase.

With a profitable company, which has quickly grown from a single shop to national brand and an important socially conscious corporate citizenship, Neal Gottlieb has a lot to be proud of with Three Twins. With all of the success he has already managed, there is still nothing which makes him happier than hearing from satisfied customers. He's built a brand people love for not only being a great product to enjoy, but the fact it does so much good for the environment as well.

Neal Gottlieb plans on continuing to make a difference, one pint at a time, for many years to come!

Three Twins Ice Cream Photo Album

Neal Gottlieb (right) with San Francisco Giants® baseball player Sergio Romo whom partnered with Three Twins for their Mexican Chocolate flavored ice cream with proceeds benefitting immigration reform

Filling pints at the factory

The interior of Three Twins' scoop shop

The exterior of Three Twins' scoop shop

Carl & Carl, Jr. – Three Twins' ice cream trucks

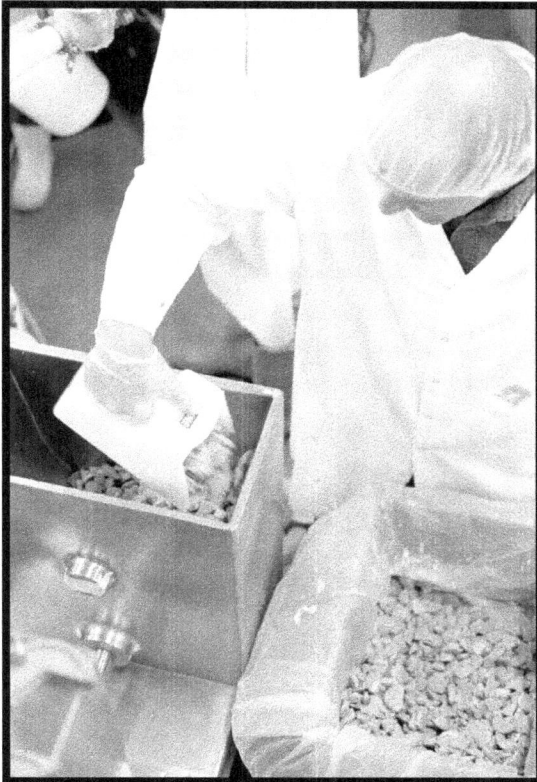

Cookies getting ready to go into ice cream at the factory

A look at Three Twins' packaging

Three Twins product lineup

Chapter 14: Ice Pops
Aiko Pops

1284 South Pearl Street
Denver, CO 80210
(303) 996 - 6400

aikopops.com
aikopops@hotmail.com

Established
2010

Leadership
Christopher Mosera, Owner/Smooth Poperator

Products
Ice pops *(Note: Popsicle™ is a registered trademark of Unilever™)*

Aiko – Japanese for "love child"…

When all of your adult relatives are either New York City firefighters or policeman, it's hard to imagine you could fall into the trap of being regarded as a "troubled youth." However, it was the path Chris Mosera was heading down. Long before 13 year-old Chris ended up getting into any real trouble, his father, a NYC policeman, took action. His father's friend owned an Irish pub. He decided, "What we have here is a failure to properly manage one's time" so he convinced his buddy to put Chris to work.

With the rationale of a few shifts of hard work would "scare him straight," Chris' father's friend had him start working at the pub as a busboy. The work was hard, but two things happened as a result of his first shift. First of all, he loved the feel and vibe of the restaurant. He found it to be fun and exciting, even though he was starting as low as you could go on the food chain in a dining establishment. Secondly, one shift in and his parents never had to worry about him getting in trouble again. From that point forward, his time and energy was dedicated to trying to get as much free time as he could to work in the pub.

After completing school, he moved from New York to Key West, a place where he could fulfill two needs: working in the restaurant business and surfing. Then he started a "bohemian/David Banner from the 70's/80's Incredible Hulk TV show" type of existence where he began moving around frequently. With his cooking skills he found getting work relatively easy, so it was simple to pick up and move. He moved from Key West to Miami, then Flagstaff, Arizona, then to Fort Lauderdale. After some time in Fort Lauderdale, Chris and two friends decided to travel across the United States. The journey ended up taking almost a year. They camped at national parks, met new people, and just had fun as they made their way to most of the 48 states in the continental U.S.

Upon completion of their trek, Chris settled in Atlanta. By this point, Johnny Cash's song, *I've Been Everywhere* sounded like a personal theme, and he decided he needed a break. Settling down might have been an overstatement, but he did want to take some time in Atlanta, and he decided to take a job in something a little more stable than the restaurant business.

Chris went to work for an international gourmet cheese distributor. This large company, representing over 1,200 cheeses from all over the world, offered more security, better benefits and a solid income for him. Plus, he liked the work. He was still in the restaurant business, just on the other side of it. Now he was introducing new cheeses and selling them to chefs and restaurant owners.

Of course, once you are in, you never totally leave the restaurant business. Chris was no exception. In his spare time he would cook for parties as a personal chef. He had dreams of retiring early, so his idea was to live off the salary from his job and then "bank" any extra revenue streams he could generate from side jobs.

Going back to his childhood with the lessons he learned from his father, Chris isn't a real fan of "down time." He found personal chef gigs tended to be at the same times: either Friday or Saturday nights. This left plenty of free time where he thought he might be able to fill in and grow his retirement fund.

One concept he had taken note of was ice pops (often referred to as popsicles™ by the public, though the name is owned exclusively by one company). There was an individual in Atlanta who was making quite a splash in the market with ice pops. Like just a handful of companies in the U.S. at the time, he was part of a growing revolution to bring the ice pop to respectability, i.e., add some flair and substance to the pops you either found caked with ice crystals on the package in the grocer's freezer or on the local ice cream truck.

The companies (in large metropolitan markets like New York, Los Angeles in addition to Atlanta) were offering premium flavors and bringing them to restaurants as desserts.

Chris loved the idea of working with ice pops. He felt there was so much you could do with the concept. You weren't limited to the sugar and water blends everyone was used to on hot summer days as a child. You could incorporate dairy, alcohol or introduce high-end fresh ingredients and spices to create a savory line.

He began to experiment and work farmers' markets. Soon, he was banking more money from selling his pops than he was with his personal chef jobs. As the two started to conflict, he looked to an old saying his grandmother used to share, "You can't have two plants and one pot of water." Knowing he couldn't do both well, he stopped offering his personal chef services and focused his spare time solely on ice pops as his career continued to grow in the gourmet cheese business.

When his company announced they were expanding and building a warehouse in Denver, they approached him to move there. He thought it would be a fun new adventure and packed up and moved again. While there, he again began selling ice pops when he wasn't working.

He found an even more voracious appetite for his pops in Denver than he had in Atlanta. He would go to a farmers' market, bring 300 pops and sell every one of them on a Sunday afternoon. He also found himself craving the work of his side business. It fulfilled both the "business side of Chris" as he states, "and the artistic side of Chris." He loved walking around the farmers' market, seeing what was fresh and buying it to make new flavors and tastes for his pop business. If watermelons were particularly tasteful and delicious one weekend, he might be buying them out and making watermelon/mojito pops the next week.

The gourmet cheese business was great. He liked the work, was making great money by this point but he was missing the "artistic fulfillment" he was finding with the pop business. He decided to put together a business plan to see if selling pops full time might be a viable option.

After formally going through the process of developing a plan, and the confidence of a product he knew he had a market for (he continually sold out every pop he could produce), he just went for it. He decided to go into the pop business full-time.

Part of his plan has always been getting the name and brand in front of the public as much as possible. While Aiko had been either the 5th, 6th or perhaps 7th gourmet ice pop company in the U.S., he was always worried some big company with deep pockets might wake up to the idea of ice pops and come into Denver. He wanted to be established enough via brand recognition to stave off competitors, even if they could outman and outspend him.

In addition to media campaigns and signage when he was out selling his pops, he began to sell wholesale to stores. Introducing his product to new customers via grocery, convenience, and specialty stores helped protect his investment in the market by getting more people familiar with his brand.

He further expanded his reach by opening a combination production facility and restaurant called Aiko Pops. His friends in the restaurant business had convinced him to offer a full menu in addition to his pops so he could build a client base even during the long Denver winters. Aiko Pops, the restaurant, opened in the summer of 2013 also offering a variety of unique soups and sandwiches.

To say his approach to the business is fluid is an understatement. Over the 3 ½ years Chris has been selling his Aiko Pops he has sold over 600 flavors. The only offering he always has on the menu is Aiko Berry, a fresh berry concoction he is always able to blend with current berries in season. Changing up his offerings is something which he loves to do. He notes he had to "retrain his palate" to be able to experiment with ice pops, though. Freezing ingredients changes the flavor profiles. The amount of cinnamon used to flavor a small cake the size of a pop is very different than the amount you would use in a pop. His years in the restaurant business were a great base of knowledge, but he truly has learned the ice pop business through trial-and-error.

Aiko Pops has provided Chris with the harmonious balance he sought by feeding both his business side and his artistic side. At this point, he's simply taking the business as it comes. Licensing, franchising, new company stores, trucks, bikes, more farmers' markets, the possibilities are almost endless.

Right now, the focus is simply on the pops and the business at hand. He turned down a major retailer who wanted to place a huge order, but would stifle some of his creativity and take his capacity (at a lower profit margin). They wanted to have him offer 6 − 8 flavors they could reorder as needed. Doing so would change his philosophy of buying and making what was fresh and available at the time, and he would either have to find a way to scale up, or sell the pops he was making at a lower price. It wasn't for him, at least not at this time.

For now, he loves introducing people to new flavors, especially if they aren't sure they are going to work themselves. One of his favorite pops to sell is his Tomato Basil. He know it never sells on its own, but if he gets the chance to speak to people, he can convince them to try it, and he's even been known to pull out his "I'll give you any pop you want if you don't like it" guarantee to convince people to give it a whirl. He proudly notes he's never given away another pop. If they try Tomato Basil, they are a fan.

Sure, out of 600 flavors there have been a few misses. When pressed he shares his experience with Truffle Popcorn. The truffle taste was a little too earthy for most, and the corn just didn't work with the other ingredients. Overall, the misses are few.

Aiko is a Japanese word which translates to "love child." This company is clearly Chris' love child. For instance, his most popular pops are his Cucumber Toasted Sesame and his Lavender Lemonade.

Now, that is uniquely Chris! Truly his love child!

It's pretty clear, these are not the sugar rush ice pops we grew up with as kids, and you won't find them at your local freezer, unless, of course, they have Aiko Pops on their label.

With Chris' rapid expansion plans in place, you may be finding Aiko Pops at a freezer near you sooner than later!

Aiko Pops Photo Album

Chris Masero

The goods: Aiko Pops

Aiko Pops is also a full-service restaurant

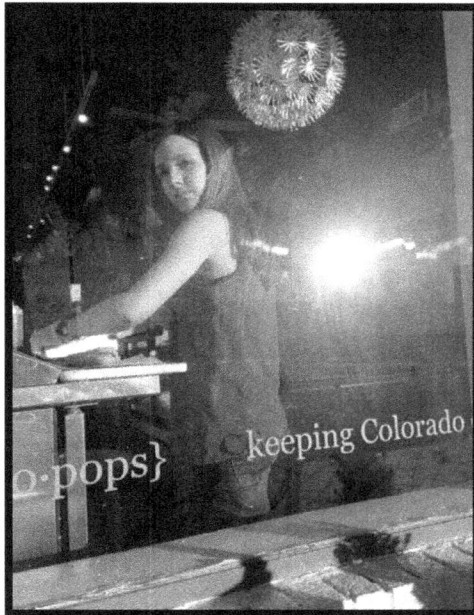

One of the most rewarding aspects of running a business for Chris is helping the local economy by providing jobs for people

Aiko Pops, the store

Aiko Pops product lineup

Chapter 15: Jam, Jelly, Marmalade and Chutney
Anarchy in a Jar

ANARCHY IN A JAR

1053 Manhattan Avenue
Brooklyn, NY 11222

anarchyinajar.com
anarchyinajar@gmail.com

Established
2009

Leadership
Laena McCarthy, Founder & President

Products
Boldly flavored jams, jellies, marmalades and chutneys

"Eat something you can connect to and think about"...

an·ar·chy (ăn'ər-kē)
n. pl. **an·ar·chies**
1. Absence of any form of political authority.
2. Political disorder and confusion.
3. Lack of any cohesive principle, such as a common standard or purpose.

Many entrepreneurs in the food industry love to talk about the "science" behind the product they are cooking up. How many of them do you think can lay claim to being an actual scientist having worked at the U.S. McMurdo Station in Antarctica?

The safe bet on that one would have to be zero.

The truth is there is one, and it's Laena McCarthy, purveyor of the boldly flavored jams, jellies, marmalades and chutneys under the name Anarchy in a Jar.

Laena worked in logistics at McMurdo providing support to scientists out in the field. Ensuring individuals have the equipment they need to conduct their experiments in the remote regions of Antarctica means you have to have a keen attention to detail. You simply don't want to leave someone stuck in a largely inaccessible location without everything they needed to be successful.

Laena spent several seasons (Sep. – Feb.) working in the Antarctic and even one winter (Mar. – Aug.) where the station largely shuts down other than a skeleton crew to work on some astrophysics experiments due to the cold and darkness.

With no infrastructure or native population, Antarctica is a unusual place to live and work. Individuals have to possess a unique mindset to be able to stay in a small community largely cut off from the amenities most of us enjoy in our daily life.

Laena fondly recalls the fact individuals are so isolated from the outside world it seemed to bring out the creative side in people. Whereas individuality can often be tied to possessions in a office environment back home (new cars, the latest phone or tech gadget, etc.), in the Antarctic it seemed to be more tied to artistic talents. People would draw, sculpt or play the guitar.

While no one is likely going to confuse McMurdo Station as a springboard to launching entrepreneurs for the food industry, Laena's time there has served her well. The attention to detail of her logistics work is something she continually draws upon. Opening yourself up to allow your creative side to come through certainly helps her as well.

Laena's journey to owning her own company began when she was born in Upstate New York. As a child her mom taught her to make jam. Clearly that factors into her story.

She went to college abroad but came back to the U.S. for graduate school. After her time in Antarctica, she was working as a digital archivist for Pratt Institute. As a hobby, she was making jams and mustards. She not only enjoyed giving the products she created to friends, but teaching them how to make these products themselves. Every conversation with someone she gave one of her homemade treats to always ended up with them stating, "You really need to sell this."

The name Anarchy in a Jar came before Laena even started her company. She would always give a tongue-in-cheek warning to friends her "non-conformist" ingredients were so pure and bold it was like anarchy in a jar. As soon as she decided to heed the calls to sell her product, the name was set from her years of using it as a joke with friends and family.

The road to starting a company in the food industry tends to be a cautiously traveled one with entrepreneurs doing a lot of research, analysis, costs studies and business plans. For Laena, it was simply a matter of writing a check to pay the set-up fee for her LLC.

While Laena didn't necessarily know the ins-and-outs of the grocery industry, she knew there was a growing demand to buying local and healthy for artisanal products with a great story. People didn't just want the same processed foods from the giant megabrands, they wanted smaller company's products. They wanted brands they could make a personal connection to based on the back story of the product and its owner.

Laena has a great story to tell. She had a quality product and she had the passion, drive and fortitude to get it on the market.

After setting up her company, her first step was testing out all of her recipes to see where to focus her efforts. She invited friends, chefs and food writers to a tasting party. Based on the feedback from the group, she landed on an initial line to offer.

With her recipes set, she went to work cooking, bottling and labeling her products. She then began to sell at a local food market. The particular market she chose was known as a hotbed for up-and-coming foods. It had caught the attention of food buyers from the local grocery stores and chains.

It was there where Laena began developing relationships with store owners and buyers. She always proceeded carefully in engaging these new opportunities. While she has liked the idea of demand outweighing her ability to produce her product, she has always wanted to build her company slowly. She never wanted the demand to so far outweigh her ability to produce her product that she would begin to get a bad reputation in the market.

Taking this approach meant she might tell a buyer to hold-off on ordering her product until she had the production capacity to meet their needs. The upfront approach with her customers has allowed her to build unique relationships with her store owners and buyers where it is a true partnership. She only takes on new clients when she knows she can deliver her products for them, and they in turn seem to have her bests interests in their efforts as well, often keeping competition at bay and protecting her market share in their stores.

The concepts of luck and timing are often cited as ways small brands succeed. This often discounts the importance of the quality of the product. The truth of the matter is without a superior product, the luck and timing factors probably wouldn't even get it on the radar. Anarchy in a Jar is a prime example of this concept.

A writer for the **New York Times**® wrote an article about Laena and her products. It was not only picked up by other newspapers, it has been the means for many other news media outlets to find her and feature her products and story. Some may write it off as a stroke of good luck or timing (being in the right place at the right time).

While she had the good fortune of being discovered by the reporter who covered her initially, her product and story are truly what got the interest of the writer to begin with, along with all of the subsequent press and TV she has received.

Her most popular flavor is her Strawberry Balsamic. Being able to enjoy it on toast in the morning, or mixing it with cheese to make an appetizer means it has the flexibility to have so many uses people seem to gravitate towards it.

Not all offerings are winners. She had a Strawberry Thai Basil offering which simply seemed hard for individuals to figure out how to use. She had a plain apple jam, and people seemed to find it a little "too boring" so she removed it from her lineup. She does offer a Spiced Beer Jelly which is also apple-based, but apparently adding beer removes the "boring" quotient as it's one of her best sellers.

Laena has been struggling to find the client base for an Arnold Palmer Jelly she has created. It's a lemon jelly infused with black tea and taste like the popular Arnold Palmer drink. Well, apparently popular everywhere but her home base of New York. People there seemingly haven't taken to the taste of the ½ tea and ½ lemonade Arnold Palmer drinks. At events and farmers' markets where people from outside of the area come to visit, she finds people love her Arnold Palmer Jelly so the jury is still out on that one.

Laena plans to continue to expand her business as she has to this point: slow and steady. She will continue to add retailers as she meets demand until Anarchy rules the world!

After Laena McCarthy's work in providing all of us "freedom from food tyranny" with her product, we may need to slightly amend the definition of anarchy:

an·ar·chy (ăn'ər-kē)
n. pl. **an·ar·chies**
1. Absence of any form of political authority.
2. Political disorder and confusion.
3. Lack of any cohesive principle, such as a common standard or purpose.
4. Bold tasting jelly, jam, marmalade and chutney produced with passion in Brooklyn, NY.

Anarchy in a Jar Photo Album

Laena McCarthy

What bottled anarchy looks like

Laena cooking

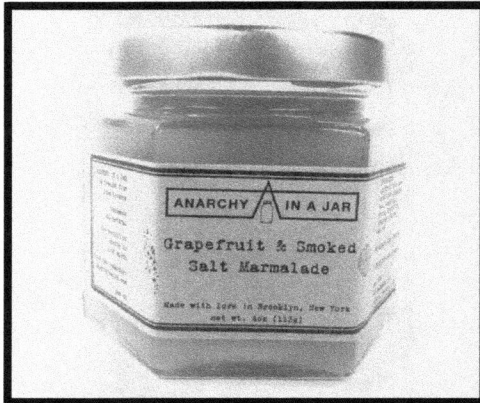

Bold flavors like Grapefruit and Smoked Salt Marmalade are what made Laena come up with the idea Anarchy in a Jar

Clementine rounds

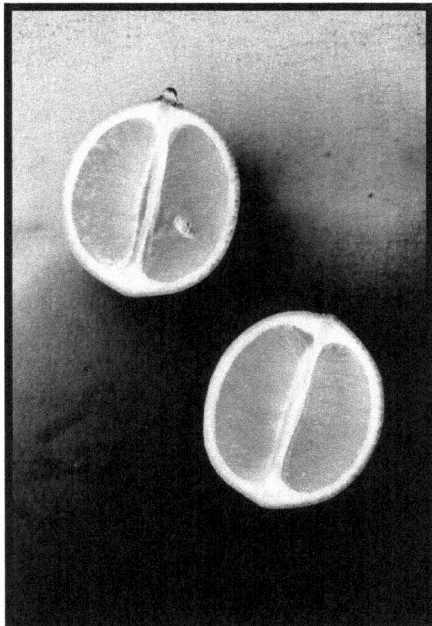

Lemons

The Anarchy crew

Anarchy in a Jar product lineup

symple ™
foods

7319 N. John Avenue
Portland, OR 97203

symplefoods.com
contact@symplefoods.com

Established
2012

Leadership
Jean-Pierre Parent, Owner

Products
Kombucha in 9 flavors, colloidal silver, sprouted, kombucha-cultured mustards and salad dressings

"Do I need to change, or do I simply need to dust off the mirror to see who I am?"...

Ask 10 people what yoga is, and you might get 10 different answers.

Is it an exercise?

Is it stretching?

Is it a state of mind?

The truth of the matter, the answer to the question of "What is yoga?" is:

"It depends."

Jean-Pierre Parent might be as well suited as anyone to weigh-in on the debate.

Jean-Pierre was born in Ohio. At the age of 16 he moved in with family friends in Texas and completed his high school education there. After graduation he began a transient period in his life where he would live in an area if it felt right, and then move on when he thought it was time to do so. He even spent some time overseas. No matter if he was living in California, Oregon, India or Hungary, he used his spare time to make the world a better place. He often helped the local community he was living in by working with Habitat for Humanity® or local orphanages.

After traveling the country and the world, Jean-Pierre settled in Portland, Oregon in 2012. He began working as a yoga instructor.

One constant in all of the locations he lived was he had made kombucha: the drink made of black tea, sugar and a probiotic starter culture. The mixture is then aged and ferments creating a tasty drink which has a long list of health benefits preached by those involved in natural and alternative medicines. Claims include weight loss; bolstering immune system; help with digestion; and even cancer treatment. The center of kombucha consumption is found in both China and Russia where it is widely used in cancer treatment.

Jean-Pierre's introduction to kombucha came in the late 80s when his mother was going through menopause. She had been struggling with hot flashes and other symptoms. Her neighbor had been talking about her own experience with kombucha. She had attributed it to putting her cancer into remission and thought it may help Jean-Pierre's mother.

Jean-Pierre's mother made her own kombucha and all of her symptoms disappeared with the first batch. Years of suffering gone in one day!

The Parent family was hooked. For the next 25+ years, kombucha has been something they have made to both enjoy as well as to continue to introduce the probiotics to their bodies.

Jean-Pierre initially began introducing kombucha on a lark to his yoga classes. Seeing some of his students rolling up their mats and heading out to their cars right after class, he got to thinking about why they were there. He thought there probably should be a social component to his classes. After all, if they weren't seeking a social aspect to the classes, wouldn't it be easier for them to simply watch a DVD at home?

With this notion in mind, he began to bring his kombucha to the classes and share it afterwards. He couldn't believe how the students took to it. Being introduced to kombucha, and developing a taste for it, many of Jean-Pierre's students began going to their local health food stores looking to buy it.

When the confused store owners would ask them where they were trying it, many of Jean-Pierre's students informed them it was from him. The stores began contacting Jean-Pierre about carrying his product. The only problem was, technically, he didn't have a "product" at that point. While he hadn't intended to launch a kombucha business, it seems he had built a market for it.

He decided to start bottling his product in a commercial kitchen and offering it for sale. He named his product Soma, which is Sanskrit for juice or nectar.

In addition to stores, Jean-Pierre also began to market directly to consumer at farmers' markets. He loved the idea of introducing individuals to something totally different which often led to surprise reactions to find it was not only healthy, but delicious.

With the reactions he got to his product, Jean-Pierre knew he was onto something. He began to put together a book lauding the benefits of organically grown foods. In all, he had a book over 800 pages long.

His mother, providing some constructive, yet critical feedback, told him there was no way anyone was going to read an 800 page book. He ended up turning it into a series of four books, entitled **Kitchen Sink Farming**. Currently, he has released the first two books in the series (**Sprouting** and **Fermenting**) and he has the other two planned for later releases (**Growing** and **Raw Food Recipes**). After all four books are released individually, he's considering putting them back together in a single compilation. (Take that, Mom!)

As Jean-Pierre expanded his product line beyond just kombucha, he launched Symple Foods as the parent company for his Soma Kombucha drink line (currently 9 flavors), his Colloidal Silver line (therapeutic immune system supplements) and his latest lines of sprouted kombucha-cultured mustards and salad dressings.

Jean-Pierre isn't just experimenting with food; he's doing a little engineering work as well. He has been developing a machine to make a kombucha concentrate. Being able to offer a concentrated product really opens up the world of kombucha to a variety of uses. Individuals could buy a concentrated liquid and add water to make their own kombucha. It could be used in healthy drinks like smoothies. He could come out with recipes incorporating a concentrated product into raw food preparation with no loss of probiotics, nutrients or flavor. There may even be an opportunity of offer individual shots of a concentrate similar to the small energy drinks commonly available in stores today. With four patents pending, it's something Jean-Pierre hopes to offer in the near future and could really help his brand.

Jean-Pierre's company follows his personal commitment and philosophy of giving back. Initially, he just offered a percentage of sales to a variety of charities.

Realizing he could be more frugal and effective by directing his resources and knowledge to those in need, he launched The Symple Fund. The goal is to offer profits from Symple Foods with the purpose of innovative solutions for problems locally and globally.

One of the first projects of the Symple Fund is to offer fermenting kits with paper and video instruction to orphanages in Africa, India and the Pacific Northwest. He's targeted malnourished children because studies show that probiotic nutrition early in life impacts the health of the individual forever. By supporting children to have healthy bodies, immune systems, and minds, he figures he can not only support their well-being, but also help kids in these key areas develop innovative strategies to contribute to global abundance.

Jean-Pierre finds the most rewarding part of his company is simply making the world a better place through something he enjoys doing and people connect with. It's been an amazing journey for him to build a company which can offer such a positive impact for individuals around the globe.

Jean-Pierre has a lot of work ahead of him to reach his ultimate goal of becoming a national brand with sales in the millions on a quarterly basis. His plans are to develop an employee-owned company as he builds it up over time.

While he has huge plans for his company, his own life plans remain simple. Should he achieve his business goals, his personal life wouldn't change all that much as his intention is to give away 95% - 98% of all profits.

The answer to why Jean-Pierre would be so generous may very well come from yoga itself. Going back to the question as to "what is yoga," Jean-Pierre has studied it extensively both in the U.S. as well as India where it began.

In the United States, yoga is a means to better yourself and your body by connecting the two together via the physical and mental aspects of the activity.

In India it's very different. In a place where they believe the spirit is immortal, connecting the mind and the body is all about acceptance of one's self and their time in their current body. They find it humorous that yoga would be viewed as a way to "make your body immortal" by using it as an exercise. For them, it's a little more existential. You aren't doing yoga to get in the perfect shape to live forever; you're using it to identify with something much deeper than just your body.

It seems Jean-Pierre's managed to parlay his love for yoga into a pretty existential existence for himself. He's got a great company, with a tremendous upside, and he's doing incredible work for those in need.

Yep, it sounds like Jean-Pierre Parent has it figured out!

Symple Foods Photo Album

Jean-Pierre Parent

Jean-Pierre keeping up on his yoga

Experimenting with formulas for mustards

Soma on the shelf

Symple Foods products are made of fresh, organic and all-natural ingredients…

Jean-Pierre focuses on this fact in his promotion of his products

Jean-Pierre's newest offering is his kombucha-cultured mustard

Symple Foods product lineup

Chapter 17: Lobster
Hancock Gourmet Lobster Co.

HANCOCK
GOURMET LOBSTER CO.
Cundy's Harbor, Maine

46 Park Drive
Topsham, ME 04086
(207) 725 - 1855

hancockgourmetlobster.com
service@hancockgourmetlobster.com

Established
2000

Leadership
Cal Hancock, Owner

Products
A full line (with a focus on lobster dishes) of appetizers, soups, entrees and desserts

Let Hancock Gourmet Lobster Co. make the "Maine" dish for your next meal…

The medical world categorizes blood types of A, B, AB and O. There isn't one mention in any medical journal of type M. If you ever have known anyone born and raised in Maine, you realize there probably should be a type M for residents of "The Pine Tree State." There is clearly something unique coursing through the veins of a true "Mainer."

Cal Hancock has a love for Maine, which clearly points to something beyond just "hometown pride." She grew up in Maine helping out in her grandmother's restaurant. It was there she not only bonded with her extended family, she developed her strong sense of being… an existence clearly entrenched in a deep-rooted sense of pride of her home state.

Nana Hazel's restaurant was operated under three driving forces:

1. They served only the finest Maine lobster.
2. They would offer the finest customer service.
3. Customers would always enjoy the best "Maine" experience.

Learning from the deep sense of "Maine-pride" her grandmother had, Cal joined her in loving everything Maine. The lobster community, in particular, important at her grandmother's restaurant and associated with the state, was one of the areas she always held with great regard.

A career in various management positions, working for companies in the healthcare and information systems industries, took her away from her home base to Ohio and Minnesota. Working for these small and large companies in various capacities and responsibilities, would serve her well later in running her own business.

Getting back to Maine and starting a business, which could give back to the state she loved, was something Cal always had planned. As she started to get serious about starting a business and moving back home, she went to a conference put on by the governor of Maine. The theme of the meeting was small business in the State.

One of the speakers was a woman who had owned a restaurant. After selling the restaurant she continued to work in the food industry by selling her lobster stew mail order. During the course of her presentation, she mentioned she was interested in selling her mail order business as well.

The presentation, along with the information about the business being for sale, really got Cal thinking. She knew her return to Maine was going to be contingent on her running her own business (she was at a point where she didn't want to work for someone else). She wasn't comfortable moving without already having the business up-and-running so this opportunity gave her a chance to start off with an established business (the woman had mentioned she had a list of a few thousand customers she sold her stew via mail order).

The more Cal thought it through, the more she knew it was right for her. She believed there was not only a demand for products made with fresh Maine lobster, it was woefully underrepresented in the marketplace. There were numerous companies which offered freshly delivered Maine lobster, but very few offering ready-to-bake products. The value-add approach would appeal to those who wanted the experience and unique flavor of Maine lobsters without the hassles and apprehensions many have in dealing with making their own meals with a live animal delivered to their door. ("Look kids, it's Pinchy the lobster… he's going to be dinner tonight.")

In the year 2000, with her professional food industry experience limited to the time in her youth working in her grandma's restaurant, Cal made an offer which was accepted to buy the mail order lobster stew business. Almost as an afterthought as they were going through the sale, the woman who was selling her the business mentioned it was going to be featured in the upcoming holiday edition of the Williams-Sonoma® catalog.

Cal truly saw the opportunity of what this meant. Sure, it was going to result in a nice bump in sales as Williams-Sonoma® has a far reach by the fans of their products and affiliations. More important than a temporary spike in sales was the value Cal immediately saw from the fact the Williams-Sonoma® team recognized the quality and taste of the product. It was worthy of being bestowed the honor of being a catalog item for the company meant Cal might have something on her hands which was bigger than she initially thought. She just had to put together a game plan to have it find its audience.

In researching ideas she came up with the International Fancy Food Show™, a yearly trade show highlighting small brands which is attended by individuals from more than 80 countries from the grocery retail, wholesale and food service industries. She wasn't quite there yet, though. She had to focus on her core business to get to the point where she could begin to go to the shows.

Her first order of business was to cater to her existing client list. Through her own cooking skills and refinement of family recipes, she came up with a few additional items to add to the lobster stew. (In addition to Nana Hazel who liked simple recipes which didn't mask the taste of the Maine lobster, she had an Italian grandmother who loved the blending of flavors so she definitely had her own unique style.) She added the new items to the mix and sent out a brochure to her mailing list.

Orders began to come in, and she started the process of building her business. As business grew, so did her product line. Soon she had built her offerings up to the point where she could send out more than just a brochure. She had officially graduated to a Hancock Gourmet Lobster Co. catalog.

By 2003 she had scaled up to the point she thought she was ready for the International Fancy Food Show™. Her newest product, a lobster pot pie was doing well so she decided to enter it into a category for judging at the show. Much to her surprise, it took first place! The award launched the company into the stratosphere. Companies at the show started ordering her product. Industry insiders not at the show began hearing about her success through trade publications, and they began ordering.

The media coverage of awards at the first International Fancy Food Show™ she attended, along with subsequent shows, led to direct consumers finding her via her website. She received coverage in print via such publications as Oprah's *O Magazine* and the *New York Times*. Her products were also featured in segments on the *Today Show*, *Good Morning America* and the Food Network™.

Her most exciting piece of media exposure came at one of the International Fancy Food Show™ events she attended. A TV producer approached her about a show on New England foods. In order to gauge whether she was worthy of inclusion on the show, they told her she would need to prepare a dish in front of an audience. This wasn't something she was real comfortable with, but she decided to give it a try anyway.

As she was making her dish in front of the audience, out walked Bobby Flay. At first, Cal thought Bobby was there to help. In her mind, he represented a welcome relief for someone stressing out by being out of their comfort zone. Bobby quickly told her he wasn't there to help; he was there to challenge her. That's right, Cal was officially challenged to a cooking duel by noted Chef Bobby Flay for his show *Throwdown! with Bobby Flay.*

Cal accepted Bobby's challenge to compete on a lobster mac and cheese challenge. It was an awesome experience and Bobby Flay was a great guy. Best of all… Cal won!

That's right, she beat one of the most accomplished chefs in a head-to-head cooking challenge. Now that's street cred!

Cal has continued to grow her business by innovating in the kitchen, promoting her business directly to customers and through publicity from the International Fancy Food Show™. In 2013 she won yet another first place award, upping her grand total over the years to ten.

In 2004 she moved from a 2,400 square foot production facility to the 6,400 square food state-of-the-art facility she resides in today. She has everything onsite including: production, customer service, operators for her mail order/internet business, back office functions, fulfillment and distribution. Though she continues to be involved in the recipes for her products, she has an executive chef and 2 other chefs to oversee the daily cooking. Williams-Sonoma® continues to be a customer carrying 25 of Hancock Gourmet Lobster Co.'s products. Delta Airlines® offers their lobster macaroni and cheese on its flights in first class meals. Her original list of direct customers has grown by thousands more.

Cal loves owning a business in Maine. She is helping out the economy and bringing jobs to the area. Best of all, she's bringing an awareness of, and spreading the passion for, Maine's lobster industry through her customers who are spread out across the United States (she is getting ready to add Canada to the mix as well).

It's safe to say Cal isn't the only one to be proud of what she's doing for Maine. Somewhere Nana Hazel is smiling. Her guiding principles remain in both her restaurant (currently being run by two of Cal's cousins) and through the Hancock Gourmet Lobster Co.

Honestly, how can the New England Journal of Medicine (it's *"New England"* for crying out loud) not recognize blood type M?

Hancock Gourmet Lobster Co. Photo Album

Cal Hancock

Cundy's Harbor

Lobster traps

Production at Hancock Gourmet Lobster Co.

Lobster Pot Pie

Lobster Flat Bread

Now that's some hardware!

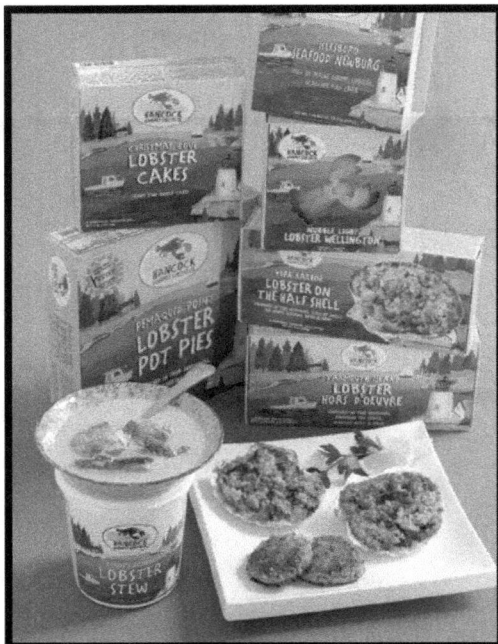

Hancock Gourmet Lobster Co. product lineup

Chapter 18: Mustard
Sun Valley Mustard

PO Box 474
Sun Valley, ID 83353
(800) 628 - 7124

sunvalleymustard.com
info@sunvalleymustard.com

Established
1984

Leadership
Joshua R. Wells, Owner

Products
Mustard in six flavors: Spicy Sweet, Chardonnay, Amber Ale, Sweet Garlic, Dill and Hot Jalapeno

Sun Valley's favorite for 30 years...

After graduating from the University of Utah, Josh Wells started working in politics. He ended up working for a U.S. Senator from Utah and later one from Idaho. In these jobs, he helped draft legislation and worked as a liaison with constituents.

After a few years of doing this, he decided to further his career by going back to school at the University of Idaho to pursue a law degree. By two weeks in, he knew a law career wasn't truly his future, but he did complete the schooling and passed the bar exam in his home state of Utah.

He practiced law for ten months before going to work in sales/marketing for a Fortune 500™ company, negotiating and administering contracts. When he got bored with the corporate life, he joined a group of software engineers to manage their intellectual property. He put his law degree to work developing their patent protections and trademarks. It was going great until the events of 9-11. With the economy instantly tightening up as a result of that tragedy, he was once again looking for work.

He ended up in real estate where he would finally find his calling. His break wasn't in the real estate business, though. The economy had negatively impacted real estate as well.

His calling came when a developer had heard he was an amateur photographer and hired him to photograph one of his properties. He was really impressed with his work and continued to use him on future projects. Soon, there was a demand for his services, and he began focusing solely on his photography.

His work began to receive recognition. This led to additional jobs and layouts in architectural magazines and digests. Despite all of the success in the world of photography, he still wanted to pursue a business to fulfill the entrepreneurial spirit which burned inside of him.

In 2011 he heard a rumor Sun Valley Mustard was for sale. Sun Valley Mustard was kind of a local institution in a city more known as a tourist destination than a place of industry. It was a perennial winner of the "Best Locally Made Products" award and the recipient of numerous national and international awards.

The business had been started in 1984 by one woman out of her garage. She built up a local following for her product by demoing it herself in grocery stores and handing it out at events like parades. She elevated the stature of Sun Valley Mustard in the community as she became a bit of a local celebrity herself.

When she decided to retire, she sold the business to an individual who seemed destined to take Sun Valley Mustard from a local favorite to something much bigger. He even got it on QVC® where the product always sold out.

Over time, the product lost its mojo and began to flounder. Sun Valley Mustard was sold again, and the third owner wasn't able to right the ship. By 2011, he too had decided to move on, and Josh Wells was able to assemble a group of investors and buy the company.

Josh realized the brand had fallen by the time he had bought it, but he didn't know how far until he really got himself immersed in it. The company was down to one employee and had stopped all advertising and marketing. Worst of all, it was being prepared in a kitchen which wasn't even certified.

Josh then fully understood what he bought was six recipes, a name and twenty wholesale customers who were still buying Sun Valley Mustard. There really wasn't anything else he could salvage from the purchase. His first order of business was to shut down production and retool the company.

Without any consumer package production experience himself, he turned to the one employee on staff to teach him how to prepare the product. He then moved the business to a new location with a certified commercial kitchen and began production again.

In order to be successful, a business owner has to be proud of his or her product. Josh wasn't a proud owner when he started selling Sun Valley again. There were some ingredients and preservatives he wanted to change in order to meet his goal of being an all-natural product without artificial flavors, preservatives or colors.

As he was looking to begin expanding his customer base, he worked a small show in Boise, Idaho. His goal was to begin selling enough product in order to generate cash flow to reformulate his recipes. Only then would Sun Valley be where he had originally envisioned.

With the need for retooling his product at the back of his mind, he didn't intend to call on the larger chains until he was ready with his final recipe. Of course, the best laid plans don't always work the way you hope they will.

Under normal circumstances, a chance run-in with a buyer of a large chain is exactly what you are looking to accomplish at a trade show. Josh had traveled to a small food show where he figured none of the big players would be in attendance. It was there he thought he could get some new accounts at smaller stores and chains.

Right there at the small show in Boise, he happened to run into a buyer from one of the largest natural food chains in the United States. She asked Josh why her stores weren't carrying Sun Valley Mustard.

Josh just put it all out there. He told the story of his purchase of the company. He spoke about changing the production facility and how he needed to rework the formula. While he didn't have anything bad in the mustard, it just wasn't where he wanted it to be at that time.

She tried his product and told him it was great. She supported his efforts to go to an all-natural product but wasn't against carrying Sun Valley Mustard in the stores as he worked through his transition. She authorized it in the stores in the Salt Lake City and Boise markets.

When Sun Valley started selling well in these stores, he called her back and asked if she could authorize his mustard in any more stores. He ended the call with authorization to add it in their Colorado stores as well.

Josh continued calling on stores, telling his story and giving out samples of his mustard. In just two years he has been able to grow the business from 20 wholesale customers to over 300 stores in five states and a sales increase of over 300% during that timeframe. Additionally, he has it featured in almost every restaurant in the area. Whether they serve burgers, sushi or fine dining, they have Sun Valley Mustard as an option.

Despite these successes, it continues to be a struggle to grow the company. The company has managed to either break even or bring in a small profit, but all of that is without Josh taking a salary. He has found the low turns of the condiment section to be a hard category in which to make a profit.

With the company entering its thirtieth year, and an owner who hasn't taken a salary in 3 years, Sun Valley is at an important time in its history. They seem to be on the right track with a rapidly growing customer base, but Josh has decided to expand the Sun Valley name, not with a new line to his product, but a whole new category. He has been busy formulating it himself. He believes it will offer greater profit margins and quicker turns on the shelf.

Where it goes from here, he isn't really sure. Through his sweat equity, he may be able to scale it up to the point where it becomes very appealing to sell it for a profit. Then again, he may continue to focus his efforts on growing the brand for the foreseeable future and keep selling as much mustard as he can by expanding one account at a time.

Josh Wells continues to experience a great deal of success in the world of architectural photography. He has generated multiple revenue streams for his work. He finally has a product he can be totally behind and proud of. He knows his mustard enhances flavors and helps people enjoy food more.

He looks forward to guiding Sun Valley Mustard to its next thirty years of success!

Sun Valley Mustard Photo Album

Josh Wells

Josh making up a batch of Sun Valley Mustard

Filling jars

Hand-labeling

History of Sun Valley Mustard
Sun Valley Mustard is the first food product manufactured in Sun Valley, Idaho. The product was placed on the market March, 1984, & since then had been a successful, profitable & growing business.

The recipe had been in the Allison family for 37 years. Lois Allison, the owner of Allison Fine Foods, had always been encouraged by friends & mustard-lovers to market her gourmet mustard. When she moved to S.V. it was her primary goal.

Josh received a written history of the company when he purchased it

From the archives: old Sun Valley Mustard labels

Sun Valley Mustard doing "its job"

Sun Valley Mustard product lineup

Chapter 19: Nuts
Bobby Sue's Nuts

65 N. Bedford Road
Chappaqua, NY 10514
(877) 554-NUTS (6887)

bobbysuesnuts.com
getnuts@bobbysuesnuts.com

Established
2009

Leadership
Barb "Bobby Sue" Kobren, Owner
Andy Kobren, CFO

Products
Nuts in the following flavors: The Original, It's Raining
Chocolate and Some Like It Hot

Coming soon to the Macy's Thanksgiving Day Parade…

While growing up in northern New Jersey, Barb Kobren not only got the nickname Bobby Sue, she also developed a love for animals. Years later, these two unrelated pieces of her Jersey-roots would be destined to come together to help form a nut company.

Barb didn't seem to be on a path to get into the nut business. This wasn't necessarily something she had always dreamt of doing while growing up, but a series of fortunate events led her to form her company which, in turn, would assist her with her passion for helping animals.

While working as the office manager and bookkeeper for her husband's dental practice, Barb began volunteering at the local Society for the Prevention of the Cruelty to Animals (SPCA) shelter. As a no-kill shelter, she was drawn to the mission of rehabilitating and helping the animals.

Initially, her work for the SPCA was hands-on volunteerism directly with the animals: cleaning cages, feeding, grooming, etc. While all volunteers continue to help with these basics, she also joined the shelter's Board and assisted with fundraising.

Any good fundraiser knows you are always looking for unique ideas and approaches to raise money for the cause. It was during a fundraising brainstorm session that someone suggested she jar and sell the nuts she gave to everyone she knew at the holidays.

Barb's nut recipe was legendary within her circle of friends and family. She hadn't developed the original recipe, though. It actually came from an aunt in Lancaster, Pennsylvania, who made them for Barb and her family when they would visit her from New Jersey in the 40s and 50s.

After expressing a fondness for this unique mixture, Barb's aunt passed the recipe along to her. Preparation involved a mix of nuts (almonds, cashews, pecans and dry-roasted nuts) covered with a spice emulsion and roasted in a convection oven. Over the years Barb had stuck to the basics of the recipe but had refined it a bit adding some flavoring of her own. People looked forward to holiday care packages of Bobby Sue's nuts.

When the idea of the fundraiser came up, it seemed only a natural to name the company Bobby Sue's Nuts. Starting out, she worked with a food chemist to refine what had originally been her aunt's, as well as her own recipes, to make them suitable for store shelves. She also did a lot of research on her own into labeling to ensure Bobby Sue's would be meeting the legal requirements to sell the product to the public.

The goal of the nut company was not only to be a profitable company but also to return a portion of all proceeds to the Westchester SPCA where Barb volunteered and served on the Board.

Once the product and packaging were done, it was time to sell. The approach Bobby Sue's took was "feet on the streets." Barb and friends knocked on doors of delis, restaurants, specialty stores and small grocery stores. These "sales reps" (read Barb and friends) would overcome objections by simply handing out samples. Once the store owners tried the product, they were interested in selling Bobby Sue's Nuts in their stores.

When she wasn't selling, Barb became a one-person public relations machine for the company. Her letters, with their story of a delicious family recipe, all natural products and a company focused on giving back to the community by helping animals, being helmed by a driven woman, made for a great story which was picked up by such notable publications as *Family Circle*, *Better Homes and Gardens*, the *New York Times* and many more.

Barb, with her "little engine that could" drive, even garnered the attention of some notable celebrities. An article about Bobby Sue's Nuts appeared on Oprah's website. Noted celebrity chef Mario Batali also became a fan. His assistant reached out to the company and inquired about buying Bobby Sue's direct to stock his home.

With all of the publicity Barb was generating, the business began to expand. To continue to grow the business, she was going to need assistance: someone with a strong business acumen and a background in finance. Luckily, her search for the perfect candidate didn't need to expand beyond the family. Her son Adam was an MBA graduate from the University of Washington and was working in the banking industry. In perhaps her greatest sales pitch, Barb got Adam to join the family business.

With Adam and his network of connections, the company continued to expand. Large retailers like Kroger® and Nordstrom's® were added along with numerous high-end hotels and specialty stores.

The growth did come at an expense, though. The larger the distribution footprint also meant thinner margins. The buying power and scope of the larger chains meant that Bobby Sue's had to keep a sharp eye on overhead and expenses.

Today, with the combination of Barb still helming the operation and Adam helping to expand the business, the future looks very promising. Barb stays involved in all of the key business decisions, large accounts and distributor relationships. Adam handles the financial side as well as targeted growth via new accounts.

The company is currently engaged in their first large-scale marketing effort: a series of "point of sale" floor displays designed to showcase Bobby Sue's Nuts in retailers.

In the company's first four years, they have managed to raise almost $40,000 for the Westchester SPCA. Their support of the organization doesn't end at the checks tied back to sales either. Bobby Sue's continues to be a large event sponsor for the organization. Plus, none other than "Bobby Sue" herself continues to support the organization by volunteering her time with the animals. With a goal of aggressive growth for the company, and new retail relationships in the works, it appears that number is going to continue to grow exponentially very quickly.

With their commitment to giving back, profitability wasn't the focus when the Kobrens started the company. It is most certainly in their long-term goals. At the four-year mark they can still be classified as a startup and as such they haven't reached the point of being able to pay salaries and deliver a profit… yet. The future will likely involve the hiring of an individual who has connections with distribution in specialty stores, or perhaps a cash infusion for growth from a venture capitalist.

Barb continues to be the visionary for the company, and her contemporaries have taken note of her efforts. Recently, she was recognized by her peers with an award for a woman-owned business from the National Association of Female Executives for both her business and community efforts.

Nothing encapsulates the future for Bobby Sue's Nuts better than when she states her ultimate vision for where the company could go. Says Barb, "The dream is a float in the Macy's Thanksgiving Day Parade. That's where I could see the company eventually ending up."

With Barb's thoughts in mind, it's pretty safe to say that the "sky's the limit" for Bobby Sue's Nuts!

Bobby Sue's Nuts Photo Album

Barb "Bobby Sue" Kobren

Adam Kobren

Making up a batch

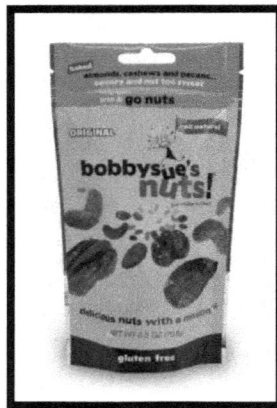

Bobby Sue's had also been sold in jars, but recently bags were added to the mix

Valentine's Day marketing

Marketing, with a tie-in to Bobby Sue's charitable work

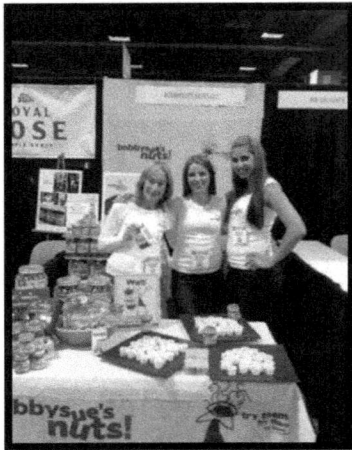

Barb (left) working a trade show

Product Line-Up

Chapter 20: Organic Flour
Daisy Organic Flour

PO Box 299
Lancaster, PA 17608
(800) 624 - 3279

daisyflour.com
sales@mcgearyorganics.com

Established
1952

Leadership
Dave Poorbaugh, President

Products
Organic flour

Putting together a business plan for the next 275 years…

Genealogy is a hobby for Dave Poorbaugh, President of McGeary Organics, the parent company of Daisy Organic Flour. He can tell you his history in this country starts in 1771 when Phillip Burbach came to America aboard the HMS Recovery. In exchange for his transport and entry to this country, Mr. Burbach spent time as an indentured servant to a Philadelphia merchant.

Phillip Burbach fought in the Revolutionary War and at some point his name was changed to Poorbaugh, likely a result of a paperwork issue, which was not that uncommon at the time. For his service, he was given land, not far from where United Airlines™ flight 93 would crash on September 11, 2001.

Much of the Poorbaugh family continues to reside in the Pennsylvania area today with most remaining in the agricultural industry. Dave Poorbaugh graduated from Penn State (another Poorbaugh family tradition) with a BS and MS in Agricultural Economics. After returning home from a stint in the Army in 1972, he went to work for Poorbaugh Grain, a grain merchant established by his uncle in 1952.

The company was an early adopter of organic farming. They were doing this before it was tagged with the name organic farming, but they became officially certified as such in 1996.

With more individuals seeking certified organic products, the company's organic grain business began to pick up. In 2000, they began to actively seek another mill to utilize for the increased production. They were struggling to find a mill to support the eastern organic farmers.

One of their conventional wheat customers was Brandt's Mill. This mill featured eight separate bins, each holding a truckload of product. This separation of the organic grains from the conventional was exactly what was needed for their certified organic processing, so they began working with the Brandt family.

The mill itself had quite a history, running back to the Herr family who owned it before the Brandt's, dating back to the 1800s. The mill had been a traditional stone grist mill until Brandt family patriarch David Groh Brandt modernized it with a steel roller system in 1907. The steel roller system created a superior product by having two steel rollers, moving at different speeds, slowly rub the wheat together. This process, known as "flouring," creates better baking flour versus the traditional stone grist mill which simply crushed the grains together.

With a mill now capable of producing their certified organic flour, McGeary brought back a historic product name they had discontinued many years before: Daisy Flour, which was now appropriately renamed Daisy Organic Flour. The "Daisy" name had been a popular moniker utilized by multiple companies in the 1800 through the mid-1900s. While there is no known reason why it was so popular, individuals like Dave Poorbaugh surmise it was simply because the daisy was the most popular landscaping flower at the time.

Almost immediately they knew they had a winner on their hands with their organic flour. David Brandt, the current family member running the mill, a person who grew up in the business, told them he could smell the difference in their product as it was being milled. It reminded him of the smell of the grains being processed when he was a child, long before the chemical fertilizers and pesticides used in today's wheat production.

Another key indicator they were onto something special was when their baking friends rolled out pie crusts. They realized you didn't need to patch them: just roll them out and go.

The response from the public was equally as impressive. Individuals began to reach out to the company, thanking them for bringing back a product their grandmothers had used. On more than one occasion, grandmothers would come in to personally thank the staff by bringing a pie they had made with Daisy Organic Flour. The sentiment most frequently shared was to thank the McGeary team for bringing back a product which allowed their recipes to "work again." The current all-purpose flours they had readily available to them at the grocery store weren't capable of making those old recipes to the quality standards of the original recipes.

In 2002, McGeary was able to secure the future of Daisy Organic Flour by purchasing the Brandt Mill. As they now owned the facility, ever the genealogist, Dave Poorbaugh began to look a little deeper into the company history. He went to the basement of the courthouse where the historical records are kept and searched. Before the Brandts and the Herrs, a family led by a man named Andrew Miller leased the land and ran a mill there. Even more amazing was the fact the land was leased from none other than William Penn himself!

Dave was able to dig up documents going back to 1740 which showed a building still on the property. Buried in the foundation of the mill onsite is a mill stone. This is an indicator there was likely a mill on the property before 1740. It looks like the Millers owned it throughout the 1700s, the Herrs in the 1800s and the Brandts the 1900s.

In Dave's research he discovered some unique information on the history of the mill. One of the most interesting pieces of information he uncovered was the fact the town of Annville, where the mill is located, sent supplies to Washington in the Revolutionary War, including flour from the Miller family.

Having a flour mill dating back to 1740 (or before) is amazing. Most of the old mills had burned because of the lack of the ball-bearing systems we have today. The friction inevitably would lead to a "fire at the old mill." The mills which survived unscathed from fire likely succumbed to an even bigger threat as improvements in modern technology made them outdated. It appears the mill always had owners who had other businesses on the property (lumber, sawmills, wool, etc.) making the mill an additional, but not their only, source of revenue.

Daisy Organic Flour, created through their unique "cool and slow," process offers a unique product to the market. As such, it tends to be very appealing to some unique segments in the market, including:

- **Heritage** – Individuals seeking to recreate old family recipes
- **Foodies** – Those who want the best foods a segment has to offer
- **Mission** – People who purposely like to buy local/buy organic
- **Allergies** – Through the internet, individuals with corn allergies have found Daisy Organic Flour, a product created in a mill where only wheat is processed

The McGeary team wants to ensure their historic mill continues to produce flour as it has for the last 275 years for the next 275 years. They are doing some great work with some heritage wheat (seeds dating back to the 1800s) both locally for their "soft wheat" as well as in Kansas where they buy their "hard wheat." This dedication to the brand means they will continue to offer the best product possible for their customers for many years to come.

One area with a lot of potential to increase the visibility of the brand is through agricultural tourism. The mill sits on a beautiful parcel in which the Quitaphelia Stream runs right through. The property sits off of Highway 422 and is only a minutes from Hershey, Pennsylvania, the home of numerous tourist attractions. The combination of historic buildings, a beautiful setting, and a working mill dating back before the birth of the nation are a potential goldmine hidden within the property.

In the world of flour, Daisy Organic remains a small competitor. For comparison, the largest competitors likely create 20 truckloads of flour a day and mid-sized around 20 truckloads a week. Daisy can produce 3 truckloads of flour in a week.

How many of those competitors can say they are the preferred flour of George Washington in the Revolutionary War, though?

Daisy Organic Flour Photo Album

Dave Poorbaugh

An old photo of the mill (Dave Groh Brandt, the person who modernized the mill in 1907 is show standing in the window right above the horse-drawn wagon)

BRANTS MILL, ON THE QUITTAPAHILLA, ANNVILLE, PA.

An old postcard showing the mill (the bridge washed away in a flood and the dam has been removed)

The mill today, shown at an open house

Miller/Plant Manager Dan Neufeld at work

You get a feel for the history when you see the old equipment at work

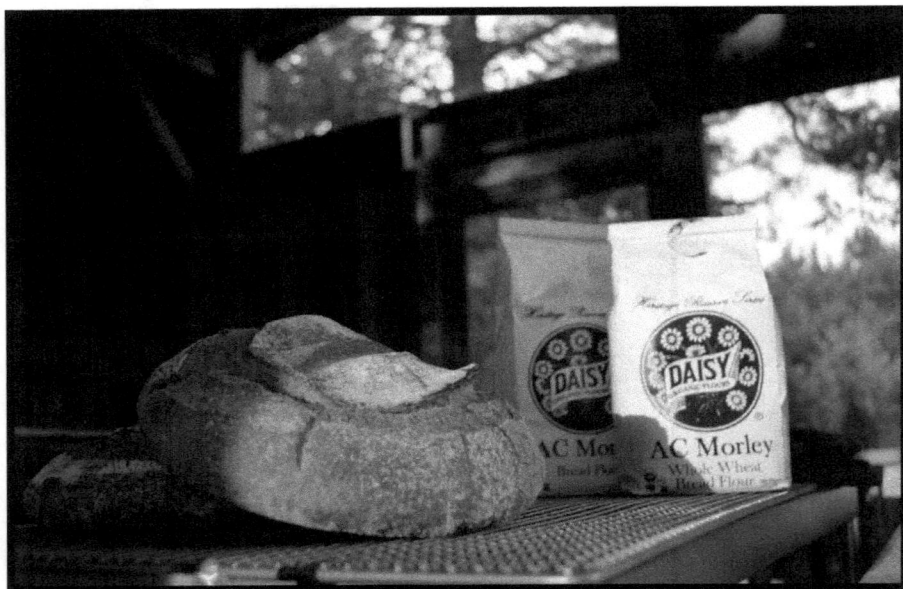

Bread baked with Daisy Organic Flour just tastes better

Daisy Organic Flour product lineup

Chapter 21: Pasta & Pizza Sauce
Casa Visco

819 Kings Road
Schenectady, NY 12303
(518) 377 - 8814

casavisco.com
info@casavisco.com

Established
1945

Leadership
Adine Viscusi, Vice President of Sales & Marketing/Owner

Products
Pasta and pizza sauces in a variety of flavors

"I'm an Italian woman. I was put on this Earth to feed people good food!"…

"Breaking through the fourth wall" is a term dating back to theater productions. It refers to acts which blur the lines between fiction and reality by having a cast member address the audience directly. The term carries over to TV and movies. Think along the lines of Ferris Bueller looking directly into the camera and discussing how to properly fake an illness to get out of school.

Adine Viscusi of Casa Visco may now be bringing the concept to print as well. There is no "voice of the author" within the chapters of **Small Brand America**, only direct accounts of small brands, and the people behind them. In a series first, we break through the fourth wall for author Steve Akley to give you a firsthand account of his interaction with Adine.

At the conclusion of our interview, Adine inquired as to where I lived. When I told her St. Louis, she said, "Well, you're not writing about my company until you've tried my product." When I protested, pointing out these are not product reviews, but stories of companies and people, she reaffirmed, "First you eat, then you write." Frightened like a child, I acquiesced, and agreed to her terms.

Sure enough, a few days later, a box showed up with six jars of awesome-looking sauces. Hmm, decisions, decisions. We decided to go with the Roasted Garlic. The Akley family is pretty savvy when it comes to Italian food since we live in St. Louis, home to The Hill (hill2000.org), a section of town with many fine Italian restaurants.

The taste… wow, I can't even do it justice. Unbelievable. I'm almost embarrassed to say, I would put Casa Visco's jarred sauce up against any of those great restaurants on The Hill. I may lose my St. Louis card for that one. Not being of Italian descent, I can't say it's better than the sauce mama used to make so trust me, comparing it to the restaurants on The Hill is the highest compliment this author can bestow.

The founders of Casa Visco were Adine's grandparents, Carmella and Joseph Viscusi, Sr. They came over from Italy and looked into either starting an independent store where they would sell Italian foods or become a wholesale grocer, distributing items to other stores. They elected to go the route of the wholesale grocery business under the name Casa Visco, which was a play on their last name (Joseph believed it was easier for Americans to pronounce than Viscusi).

Casa Visco would buy items in bulk and either sell them directly or rework them to sell (for instance, they bought raw ingredients like bread crumbs, parsley and cheese to make seasoned bread crumbs under the Casa Visco name). With Carmella and Joseph, along with sons Mickey and Joe helping out, the Viscusis built up a large client list comprised of both Italian specialty markets and traditional grocers.

One of the greatest gifts an Italian family can bestow someone is their pasta sauce. The sauce is often a glue which bonds the family. Sunday dinners are a time families like the Viscusis spend together cooking, eating and sharing the details of their lives. Throughout the course of these weekly events, the sauce is simmering in the background creating the unique smells and tastes which become associated with these best of times.

Carmella wanted to provide the ultimate Italian display of affection by sharing this sauce with her customers so she and Joseph jarred up some of the sauce she made from the tomatoes in her garden for their customers at Christmas one year. It truly is like saying you are part of the family because they were sharing the unique tastes the Viscusi family would enjoy with those Sunday dinners.

The next time Joseph was making his rounds to fill his customer's shelves, he was getting orders for the Viscusi family sauce. The only issue there being he didn't actually sell the sauce. It was just a gift, a way of saying "thank you for your business." Based on the feedback and demand they had already created, he and Carmella knew they had to start offering her unique recipe under the name Casa Visco.

In the basement of their small bungalow-style home, Carmella and Joseph began making and jarring their sauce. Soon the demand was so strong for the sauce, they had to expand. The bought a van and parked it in their driveway. It became the "warehouse."

When the business became too big for the bungalow and van-warehouse, they moved into a true production facility where Adine remembers these very old Italian women cooking sauce in 50 gallon pots over open flames and then jarring, capping and labeling each bottle by hand. The business became a true family affair with Carmella and Joseph, their children and 12 grandchildren, all helping out. Adine recalls the great fun she had working as child alongside her cousins and extended family at Casa Visco's production facility/distribution warehouse (they continued to stay in the wholesale grocery business as well).

When Adine was just four year old, Joseph, the patriarch of the family, died. Carmella retired from a daily role at Casa Visco but stayed closely involved in the running of the business at daily post-work meeting at her house. There, the men in the family would meet, where she would dote over them, and they shared what was happening at work.

With a strong regional brand in their pasta sauces, the Viscusi family began to think about focusing solely on their sauce line and selling the wholesale grocery business. After much discussion at the post-work "happy hours" and Sunday dinners, and with Carmella's approval, that's exactly what they decided to do.

After working at the family business all through her childhood, Adine worked a series of jobs outside of Casa Visco starting as soon as she could legally get a non-family job. She started in fast food at 15. She then worked in a clothing store. As she began searching for what she might do, she took a correspondence course through the mail on gemology through the Gemological Institute of America™. She used her knowledge by working in a jewelry store. Then she worked as a cocktail waitress while going to Hudson Valley Community College. It wasn't until she was ready to move out of the house, facing regular rent bills, she began to seriously look at coming back into the family business her father was now running.

Through the leadership of three generations, Casa Visco has maintained a trajectory of growth with its pasta sauce by a commitment to the quality and homemade-style production. The national brands inject steam to pasteurize and cook their sauce quickly.

Casa Visco won't have any of that.

Instead, they use only fresh ingredients, and they cook their sauce low and slow. Just like the Viscusi family has always done at those Sunday dinners. The end result is a complex layering of flavors which cannot be recreated via faster cooking methods.

Their expansion has also been "low and slow." They have been systematically increasing distribution and expanding their reach over time. They haven't attempted to ramp-up too quickly which might have led them to try to take shortcuts to reach a larger audience.

The results are impressive. Their Schenectady, New York-based company has solid brand recognition in the Northeast. Their pizza sauce is the number one selling direct store delivery pizza sauce in New England only trailing behind Ragu Pizza Quick™, which is a much larger brand with far-reaching distribution and a huge advertising budget.

Adine Viscusi lists the fact she is providing hearty, wholesome and good food to her customers as the favorite part of her job.

She states it best when she says, "I'm an Italian woman, I was put on this planet to feed people good food."

This follows suit with Adine's role of Sales & Marketing she also fills for the company. She loves to get out to stores and demo the product. Her personal mantra is, "Put in mouth = put in cart." (Note that this follows suit to her, "Eat first, then write" orders she gives to people writing books about her company.)

The future seems to be now for Casa Visco. They are looking to introduce one-pot meal makers and pizza kits which include their sauce and a pizza dough which was perfected by Adine's father (he recreated it at the bakery they are working with, and they have been able to produce it on a large-scale basis).

In addition to expanding their brand in the U.S., they are also growing internationally. They are already exporting to China and are looking for future growth via countries like Japan, Korea and Brazil.

There's even a family in St. Louis who has scrapped their weekend plans to head to The Hill to enjoy some of the local fare. Instead, they are cooking pasta at home. It feels like a Red Wine Sauce night tonight.

Thanks Adine!

Casa Visco Photo Album

Adine Viscusi

Carmella and Joseph Viscusi (this painting of them is displayed on the walls of Casa Visco Headquarters)

Adine wearing her VP of Sales & Marketing hat leading a demo

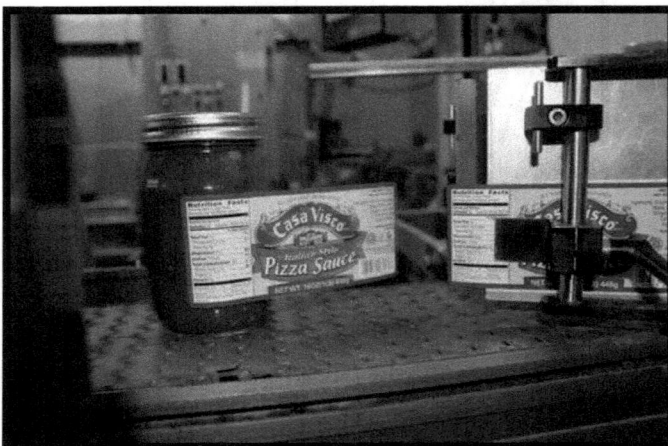

Pizza sauce going through the production line

Casa Visco is actively involved in giving back to the community

Casa Visco on display

A legacy photo of the Casa Visco team showing their products

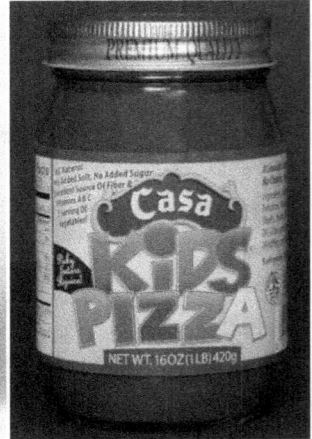

Samples of Casa Visco's product lineup

Chapter 22: Salsa
The Brooklyn Salsa Company

Brooklyn, NY
(404) 409-7852

bksalsa.com
info@bksalsa.com

Established
2008

Leadership
Rob Behnke, CEO and CoFounder
Matt Burns, Creative Taste Operator and CoFounder

Products
Salsa in the following flavors: The Pure, The Green, The Tropical, The Curry, The Hot and The Mole

Livin' la vida salsa…

Though it is correctly identified as a condiment, there have been instances where individuals have been known to debate whether salsa is, in fact, a condiment or a dip. Rob Behnke and Matt Burns, Co-Founders of The Brooklyn Salsa Company, add yet another twist to this discussion. They make the case for salsa being a *lifestyle*. When you hear their story, your vote may swing to the lifestyle corner as well.

Neither Rob or Matt were born and raised in Brooklyn, though you wouldn't guess that if you didn't know their history. They have become part of their beloved borough through an appreciation for the local culture, food and multiple avenues for their creative and artistic outlets.

Rob grew up in New Jersey. He moved to Brooklyn to pursue his passion as a musician. Being in the area afforded him the luxury of being able to work a job during the day (selling ad space), combined with plenty of opportunities for him to find work with his band.

Matt Burns grew up in South Dakota. His first job was at a local taqueria where he held a variety of positions. When he began cooking, he found he really had a strong interest in creating fresh salsa. Not only did it fit his vegan lifestyle, he was amazed at the simplicity of developing rich flavor profiles by working with the ingredients. His interest in salsa was strengthened when he began working at an organic farm and could really experiment with a variety of fresh ingredients.

Like Rob, Matt was a musician, but he had another interest as well: acting. Knowing that the window to break into the acting business is fairly short, he decided to make the move to New York to see if he could find work.

The same time Matt was moving to New York, Rob was advertising for a roommate on Craigslist®. Matt answered the ad, and the two hard-working artists not only became roommates, but friends as well.

Living in a loft apartment in a converted old opera house afforded a tremendous opportunity for a couple of individuals in the local art world. The building contained a basement where shows could be put on for 100 – 150 people. It was at one of these shows where Rob's band and a few others were playing. Matt had prepared some homemade salsa he was sharing with guests. One of their close friends in passing said it was so good they should start a business by bottling and selling it.

Back at his job the next day, Rob spent the entire time thinking about the comment. Could there be a business opportunity selling salsa? When he got home, he told Matt he really thought they should pursue the idea of bringing his salsa to consumers.

They proceeded to the rooftop of their building and just started talking. With a backdrop of the city of Manhattan, they literally shared ideas to make it work and formulated a plan to move ahead.

Starting from scratch, without a consumer packaged goods background, you cannot simply flip a switch and be in business. Without a substantial cash infusion from investors, it is extremely challenging to even enter the food business much less hope to have any degree of large-scale success.

Rob and Matt began a tactical approach to slowly reaching the market; one that would afford them the luxury of maintaining control of their brand and not have to seek outside investment in which they would be losing an ownership stake as well.

Their first step in bringing Brooklyn Salsa to market was to generate capital. They did this by creating a food delivery business with dishes that featured their salsa. The product was so good, they immediately gained a large following in the area. Being that they were operating illegally, they knew this wasn't a long-term solution but instead were using their delivery business as sort of a gold rush to generate the revenue they would need for the second phase of their plan.

The second phase of their plan was simply to generate a buzz and interest in The Brooklyn Salsa Company, even when it wasn't yet on the market. They used local shows and events to give their product away. They also became active in business groups where they would discuss their product and share samples. The feedback was the same they had received each step of the way to that point: The Brooklyn Salsa Company was infinitely better than any product they could buy in the stores. They had created a demand for a product that technically didn't even exist at that point.

One of the contacts they developed through their networking was an individual in a nationwide chain. Through this person, Matt and Rob were offered the opportunity to launch their brand exclusively through their stores. While this was certainly an incredible opportunity, it wasn't right for Matt and Rob at the time. Tying their product to one store wasn't the vision they had. Even though they passed on the deal, it did offer them an incredible entrée to getting into other retailers.

With the buzz they created, as well as the nationwide interest from the well-known chain, Rob and Matt began selling their product on their own. It was June of 2010, two years after their rooftop meeting to lay out their plans, and The Brooklyn Salsa Company was officially in business.

Selling and delivering in their company car, a Prius®, Matt and Rob began getting customers: 1 store, then 10 stores, then 20. By the end of their first year, they were in over 100 stores. Calling on store managers, delivering product, stocking it, running demos, as well as making the actual salsa, meant those 100 stores were about the capacity the two could handle on their own. The good news was the sales numbers now being generated by those stores meant they were successful enough to garner attention from distributors.

With the power of the channels to market through the distributors, combined with a product that offered fresh ingredients not genetically modified, Brooklyn Salsa began to grow very rapidly. Consumers raved about the difference in taste versus what they were used to getting from the national brands.

There are several factors which give The Brooklyn Salsa Company's products its taste advantages over its competitors. The first is the fresh produce used in creating it. Not utilizing dehydrated product instantly gives it a totally different taste experience that consumers are used to with the usual brands you find on grocer's shelves.

The second is the fact it's real food with no preservatives. Rob and Matt work with local organic farmers as well as city co-ops and community gardens… even local school gardens to make their product. When you are sourcing from the same places consumers get his or her own homemade salsa ingredients, it is going to taste like food they can relate to. This isn't always the case when you are dealing with genetically modified ingredients found in national brands.

The third component, and wildcard to the whole equation, is Matt. He is simply a creative genius in putting together unique flavors which really work well together. He is always pleased when he hears from someone who starts a conversation by saying, "I don't normally like curry, but I tried your curry salsa..."

The appreciation Matt and Rob have for Brooklyn goes beyond just what it affords them in terms of a place to live, work and follow their passion and dreams. It's a relationship they reciprocate by giving back to the local community. They are actively involved in teaching youths and urban gardeners about the benefits of city gardens. They offer instructions on rooftop gardening, school gardens, and neighborhood co-ops. Often, these teaching opportunities end up forging relationships which in turn develop into business partnerships for the salsa business.

Their business sense is steeped in the principles of conscious methods in their approach to business. They accomplish this goal via direct trade with farmers, buying local, and affiliating their company with farms utilizing organic farming.

Today, VIP diners at the Barclays Center® in Brooklyn, enjoying a Nets™ game or a concert, may order Brooklyn Salsa. Through their network of distributors, The Brooklyn Salsa Company is now in more than 1,000 stores across the United States, and their product can also be found in Japan, Thailand and London. Seeing the benefits of maintaining control at the local level, Matt and Rob have started to take back distribution in the immediate area surrounding their home base. This allows them to maintain direct relationships with the stores where their active involvement can assist in establishing partnerships with stores to grow their business.

Their list of business alliances continues to grow as well. Currently, they are working cross promotions with fashion designer Gant Rugger® (*gant.com*), King's County Distillery® (*kingscountydistillery.com*) and noted chefs, the Sussman brothers (*thesussmanbrothers.com*).

Matt and Rob are perhaps most proud of the fact that their salsa still affords them the benefit of bringing their artistry to their product. They have taken painstaking efforts to make their product not only a unique flavor experience but to make it aesthetically pleasing as well. Their jar designs, with their bold colors, are like works of a great artist when stacked up next to each other.

Of course, there is the whole existential approach they adhere to in conveying salsa as a lifestyle. The fact that salsa is a shared experience, with individuals gathering around a communal bowl, is a powerful driver to continue to produce the best product possible for their customers. They also take a lot of personal satisfaction from the fact these shared experiences are made possible from their dedication to delivering the highest quality ingredients with every jar. Phrases like "salsa powered" and "take the lid off" aren't just catchphrases or buzzwords. They are truly drivers for Rob and Matt to continue to push themselves and their company to reach new heights and deliver new experiences to new fans as they continue to grow their company.

The Brooklyn Salsa Company Photo Album

Matt Burns & Rob Behnke

CONSCIOUS METHODS ™

DIRECT TRADE

LOCAL SOURCE

ORGANIC FARMERS

Guiding principles used by the Brooklyn Salsa Company

Solar power!

The crew working at the Hepworth Farm

"Salsa plants"

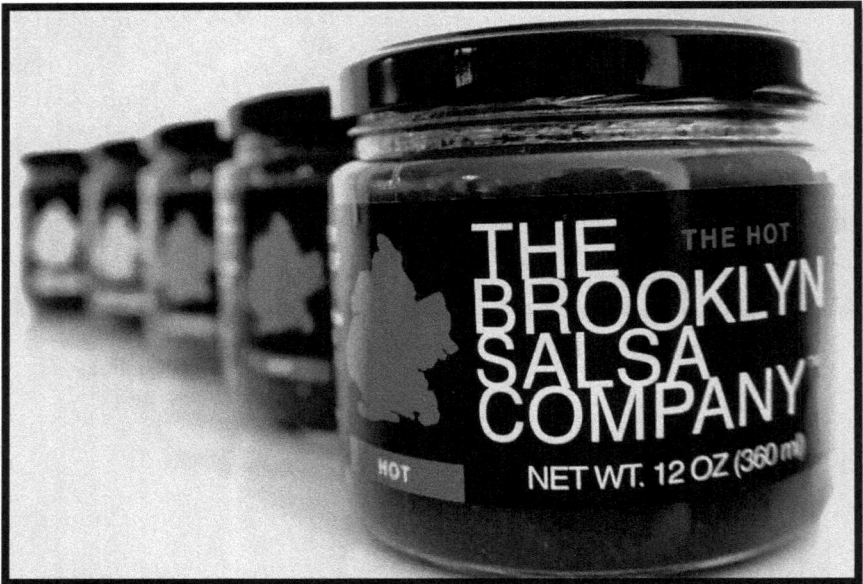
The Brooklyn Salsa Company product lineup

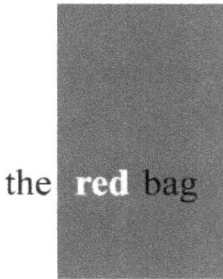

P.O. Box 1873
Big Bear Lake, CA 92315
(909) 584 - 8267

sarkisiancoffee.com
debra@sarkisiancoffee.com

Established
2000

Leadership
Debra Sarkisian, President

Products
Specialty coffees in various roasts, blends and flavors

The greatest comeback story in the history of small brands…

Everybody loves a comeback story. In the world of small brands, a comeback isn't usually in the cards. On the positive side, launching a small brand can end in one of three ways:

1. The business does enough to sustain itself over time (simply holding its own).
2. The brand does well enough it unofficially transitions from small brand to large brand, and maybe a megabrand if everything falls into place.
3. The company becomes large enough, or perhaps fills the void of a larger company, and it ends up getting bought out.

Unfortunately, the success stories are far outweighed by the non-successes. It's fun to talk about the winners, but the flipside is often pretty bleak: loss of business, personal wealth and complete financial devastation. (Yikes!)

With all of the hurdles a small business has to clear, it's amazing any can withstand the challenges they face and find the successes outlined in the list above. Perhaps this is what makes *Small Brand America* such a great read (Note: there hasn't been such an effective use of affirmation marketing as you just saw there since Dial® developed the company's, "Aren't you glad you used Dial®, don't you wish everyone did?" campaign.)

Thinking about all of these issues really puts into perspective to what Debra Sarkisian has gone through to be involved in two success stories from the world of small brands. Failure wasn't something Debra could even fathom. After all, her involvement in the both businesses she would helm all went back to a promise she had made to her father.

For the Sarkisians, their introduction to the world of coffee came in 1971 when Debra's father, Wally Sarkisian, started a small specialty coffee company. He had a successful career in the grocery business which included owning a grocery store at one point. Over time, he had started his own food brokerage where he would represent other company's products in stores and called on company headquarters to promote these brands.

He never felt really comfortable doing this, though. In the food brokerage business, you are always one step away from difficult times as brands often change affiliation with brokers as a means to step up the profile of their products. The national companies often seem to believe food brokers really pay attention to their newer products but once the honeymoon period is over, they then pay attention to the next new item in their catalog.

Wally always believed adding something tangible to the mix, something he owned, would be a more stable way to approach the business. His idea was totally unique to the time: specialty coffee.

This may be almost laughable now, but in 1971, the megabrands didn't just dominate, they *owned* the category. Over time there has been a resurgence in the world of coffee. It's probably not uncommon today to see specialty coffees equal or even exceed the traditional brands which were exclusively in cans, at that time. Now, specialty brands are the trendsetters. Stores seemingly have changed overnight where the specialty coffees are used to fill their shelves. They aren't just small companies, either. Large, well-known entities like Starbucks®, Peet's® and even the megabrands have entries on the market.

So here is Wally Sarkisian, looking to start a new category in what was considered a mature segment in the grocery industry. He was an Arcadia, California-based, Chicago transplant, with no ties to the world of coffee.

This can't happen, can it?

Well it did. To figure out exactly how, you would have to have known Wally Sarkisian. He was an incredible salesman whose affable personality got him the entrée he needed into the relatively small world of coffee. Once you are "in," you are one of them, and since it seems everyone knew each other in the coffee business, he had plenty of people pointing him in the right direction to get his coffee company started.

Once he had the supply chain down, Sark's Supreme was born. He had the means to sell and distribute his brand: himself. He already had the contacts in the grocery industry from his food broker company, so it made complete sense to work with his existing customers to get his own brand going.

Megabrands pay mega-dollars to focus groups to develop packaging and come up with unique branding and marketing ideas. They didn't have Wally Sarkisian, though. Wally came up with his own ideas to sell his product. The first was his bright red bag. The candy apple red bag could be seen across a store. It stood out like a beacon and screamed, "Put me in your cart," to consumers.

The other genius idea Wally came up with was unique shelving to help stock and display his bagged product in a section of the grocery store where only canned coffee could be found. He didn't know it at the time, but his idea was to create a specialty coffee section "within the section" of coffee.

Again, this is second nature now. There isn't a store set in a grocery store of any size which doesn't have a specialty section, often highlighted with some pre-fab specialty coffee shelving unit.

Wally was coming up with ideas on his own, so he didn't have "pre-fabricated" units in which to place Sark's Supreme. Nor could he afford to get something designed. Luckily, you can add "handy" to Wally's marketing genius and ace salesperson monikers. Wally would overcome not having the units he envisioned by custom building them onsite at the stores. He'd go in with raw materials, a series of screws, a standard saw, a miter saw and a grinder and go to work. He'd leave the store with not only a beautiful area which would showcase his product, but he had a section of real estate on those shelves which he owned, only to be filled with those beautiful red bags of coffee.

Brilliant!

Debra had joined her father early on, helping out filling store shelves and assisting in the build outs of those shelving units. Her mother was actively involved in the business as well serving the back office functions to Wally's work in the fields.

In 1980, after a store set out in the desert, Wally had a frank discussion with Debra. In the car on the way home, he turned to 19 year old Debra and said, "If anything ever happens to me, you have to keep this coffee company going for your mom."

A horrified Debra wanted clarification. Wally assured her there was nothing wrong with him, and he wasn't going to die, but in life you never know when your time is up, and he just wanted Debra's assurance she would continue what he had done in order to keep the brand going and provide for his family. With a sigh of relief, Debra gladly promised her father she would do exactly that.

Unfortunately for the Sarkisian family, two weeks later Wally passed away. True to her word, Debra immediately jumped into the family business, and she and her mother Rose, as a team, kept it going. Despite a steep learning curve, they literally were able to keep all of the commitments Wally had made to his customers (the most unbelievable being the fact Debra stayed up all night at a store set the night before her father's funeral so as not to damage the reputation of Sark's at a set Wally had committed to be a part of).

Not knowing the business like her father, there were bumps in the road for sure, but Debra and Rose kept at it, and the brand continued to thrive. Eventually, in 1987, she had built it up to a point where the company had caught the attention of one of the largest consumer goods brands in the world, and they bought out Sark's Supreme. Debra had fulfilled the promise she made to her father, and the money from the sale ensured her mother would be taken care of for the rest of her life.

The megabrand had bought the coffee blends, they bought the packaging, and even the distribution channels, but they didn't get Wally, Rose or Debra Sarkisian. Without their careful attention to the brand, over time it began to decline. By 1999, they had taken the product off of the shelves and sold off the name (it wasn't then, nor is it now, being produced).

After selling off the coffee brand, Debra had continued with the food broker company and also kept pretty busy with her family. She had 5 children over that time frame as well.

Over the years, people had continued to ask her if she was going to bring back a coffee line or start another company. Because she didn't have time, and because she had signed a ten year non-compete clause when she sold out, she really couldn't bring it back even if she had wanted to.

Now, with Sark's Supreme off the shelf, she started to reflect on what her father had told her in the car out in the desert so many years before. "If anything happens to me, you have to keep this coffee company going…"

Had she kept her promise?

Of course she had, but still, she couldn't help but think about what if she started another coffee company? If she did, she could, in fact, keep the coffee company going as her father had wanted her to do. Doing so would mean she was starting where her father had (as an outsider in the world of coffee), and in a much more competitive landscape (they no longer would be the sole representation of specialty coffee on the shelves).

In 2000, Debra took the leap and got back into the world of specialty coffee under the family name of Sarkisian.

Starting all over isn't like simply hitting a reset button. She had to develop her own entrées into the world of coffee, but just like her father had found, once you navigate your way in, there are plenty of people willing to help you out. Customers who remember Sark's Supreme were excited about the coffee in the red bag coming back, even if it had a slightly different name.

Getting back in hasn't been easy. For instance, it took Debra three years to get into Ralph's®, the first chain she attempted to work her way into. Once she was in Ralph's®, she has been able to secure distribution into Kroger®, Albertson's®, Safeway® and Wal-Mart®. An impressive list to be sure.

It's been rewarding and a key driver for Debra to know how happy her father would be to see that red bag back on the shelf in such well-known, and respected, companies.

Debra promises to continue to grow the company by offering a top quality product at an affordable price. It's pretty easy to believe she's going to make it happen. She's not one to go back on a promise, even if she has to deliver on it twice!

Sarkisian Specialty Coffee Photo Album

Debra Sarkisian

Wally Sarkisian

the red bag is back!

Consumers remembered the red bag Sark's Supreme had been packaged in and it became a big part of the relaunch for Sarkisian

Sarkisian booth at a trade show

Two generations of specialty coffee expertise:
Rose and Debra Sarkisian

Sarkisian product lineup

Chapter 24: Toothpaste
Theodent

1441 Canal Street
New Orleans, LA 70112
(504) 264 - 5050

theodent.com
info@theodent.com

Established
2007

Leadership
Dr. Arman Sadeghpour, President and Chief Executive Officer
Dr. Tetsuo Nakamoto, Chief Science Officer and Chairman of the Board

Products
Rennou-based toothpaste (an alternative to fluoride)

Focusing on the positive…

A quick internet search of the word "fluoride" provides some interesting results. There is an overwhelming amount of information on the positives and negatives of fluoride use. Certainly more on the negatives, but it is the internet after all, who knows how accurate any of it really is.

The most interesting hits from a fluoride search are the conspiracy theorists. Apparently, the government is regulating our fluoride intake. Of course, this allows "them" ("them" being the open-ended internet version of the word) to control our minds and actions.

The Theodent team doesn't waste any time on internet searches for the word fluoride. They have developed a product called Rennou which is the active ingredient in their Theodent brand toothpaste. Through their clinical work, they have found Rennou to not only provide greater protection for teeth as well as two key differentiators:

1. Unlike fluoride which just protects teeth, Rennou actually helps regenerate enamel making it even better for long-term dental health.

2. Rennou is safe to consume. Internet chatter aside, every tube of toothpaste with fluoride has a government mandated warning talking about the dangers of consuming fluoride.

All of Theordent's marketing and promotions hinges on those two facts. They love to talk about positive impact their toothpaste has on your teeth, and the fact it is completely safe… which seems to be something many people are interested in since all toothpaste goes in your mouth, particularly if children are involved.

Despite the great story they now have to tell, and the fact Rennou had been discovered over twenty years before it came to market, it's almost amazing to think it took a series of unrelated coincidences, and a national tragedy for Theodent to make its way onto store shelves.

It wasn't a government conspiracy keeping Theodent from making the journey from research grant to consumer product for over twenty years. In the late 1980s, Dr. Tetsuo Nakamoto and the mother of Theodent President and CEO Arman Sadeghpour did a joint research grant on the impact of caffeine on prenatal teeth.

Not surprisingly, they found caffeine stunted bone growth. They also checked two similar compounds, one of which was theobromine, the natural extract found in the cacao bean, commonly used to make chocolate. Perhaps, the biggest finding from the study came from the fact theobromine actually helped regenerate bone growth and not inhibit it.

When the study was completed, the research wouldn't be reevaluated until years later when Arman Sadeghpour was working on his PhD at Tulane University in New Orleans. Since his high school days, in his spare time he would work in the lab of Dr. Nakamoto, his mother's old colleague.

He had already started on his thesis when New Orleans was tragically struck by Hurricane Katrina. Like much of New Orleans, Tulane was severely damaged by the storm. The university closed to rebuild. The individuals Arman Sadeghpour was working with on his research had left, and his work-to-date was lost.

He turned to his mentor Dr. Nakamoto for suggestions. Dr. Nakamoto thought the perfect topic for a thesis would be for Arman to dust off the old research he had done with Arman's mother.

Arman Sadeghpour was able to expand the research from the impact of theobromine on neonatal bone to the impact on teeth.

His work led to not only his PhD, but the structure for a business bringing a consumer product to market.

In 2007, Dr. Arman Sadeghpour and Dr. Tetsuo Nakamoto went into business, bringing Theodent, the brand name for toothpaste containing the active ingredient they called Rennou (a compound made from the theobromine found in cacao plants).

Forming the company was just the start for them, though. They still had a lot of work to do.

- They had to secure all of the intellectual property associated with Theodent. They knew they had a revolutionary product on their hands, which meant established competitors would be coming after them. The better protected they were up front, the easier time they would have protecting their research and intellectual property.

- They needed to develop the product themselves. This went beyond just formulating the ingredients; they needed packaging and a manufacturing facility.

- The final component was a strategy for getting their product into the hands of consumers.

Once their research was locked down with the appropriate patents and trademarks, they secured the brand image. The tie-in to the cacao bean, and in turn chocolate, was a natural way to connect with consumers. Everyone loves chocolate and being known as the "chocolate toothpaste" was a good thing, even if their product was really derived from the cacao bean and not actually chocolate. They embraced the whole notion of the chocolate toothpaste by developing a box for the product which even had the look of an old-time chocolate bar packaging.

Their goal to get their product to market was simple: they were going to be a higher-end toothpaste. The production runs of their product as a start-up versus their competitors' runs, which numbered into the thousands or hundreds-of-thousands, dictated they would never be able to compete on price, so they elected to make Theodent better than any product on the market in every way. Their tube is better quality than anything you will find on store shelves. The end is capped with a tapered metal tip. The design on the tube is so elegant they hear from consumers who love the fact they can leave their toothpaste on the counter and not have to worry about putting it away in a drawer.

Today, Theodent has three products in their line. Their Classic is a mild spearmint flavor. They offer a children's version (called Kids) which is chocolate in taste. The company also offers Theodent 300, which is an extra-strength spearmint-flavored version of their classic line.

While the Classic and Kid's lines retail in the $10 - $15 range, Theodent 300 retails $99.99 and is only available through select dental and medical offices and their website. One might wonder who would buy a $100 tube of toothpaste, but the strong sales of the product are a clear testament to the fact it helps people in need. Individuals with medical conditions, prohibiting saliva generation (either hereditarily or through medical issues most often tied to radiation treatment of cancer), often have enamel issues, and Theodent 300 has become a popular way to combat the loss of enamel as a result of these medical conditions.

The future of the company looks as bright as a Theodent customer's smile. Whole Foods® took the very unusual step of making Theodent available nationwide. Their typical wholesale approach involves regional distribution, and brands which can organically grow by region are expanded upon over time. Theodent Classic and Kids lines were both immediately made available to customers across the country.

Retailers aren't the only ones to take notice of Theodent's success. Competitors from the traditional fluoride-based brands have contacted them as well. If a mutually beneficial agreement can be worked out, Theodent's management team is not opposed to a licensing agreement for Rennou.

Toothpaste hasn't changed much since fluoride was introduced to the product in 1917. Sure, there are new flavors, textures and few new tube styles, but the base product has remained basically the same.

Theodent offers the first innovation to toothpaste in almost 100 years. Based on the findings of both Dr. Sadeghpours (Arman and his mother) as well as Dr. Nakamoto, we may be at the dawn of a new era of dental care.

A world dominated by "chocolate toothpaste" sounds like a pretty great place to be!

Theodent Photo Album

Dr. Arman Sadeghpour

Dr. Tetsuo Nakamoto

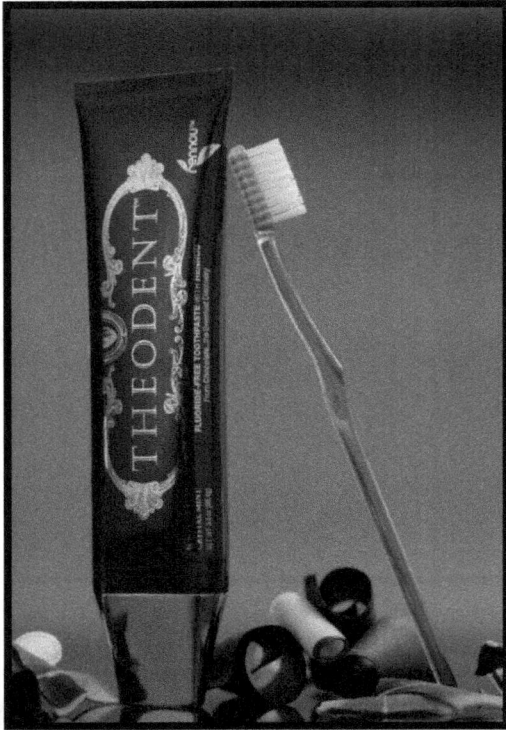

Even though the product is made from a derivative of cacao and not actually chocolate, it connects with consumers and plays heavily into their marketing of the product

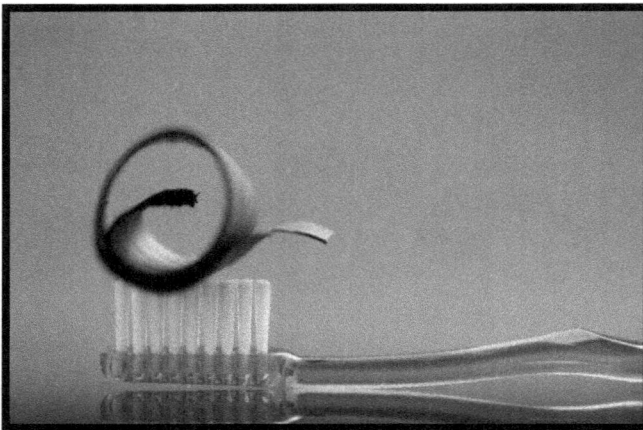

The "chocolate toothpaste"

Their elegant packaging is meant to be left on the counter and not hidden in a drawer

Getting an endorsement from the tooth fairy was pretty big for the Theodent team

OUT WITH THE OLD...IN WITH rennou™

Rennou… the key ingredient in Theodent

Theodent product lineup

Chapter 25: Veggie Burgers & Veggie Bites
Hilary Eats Well

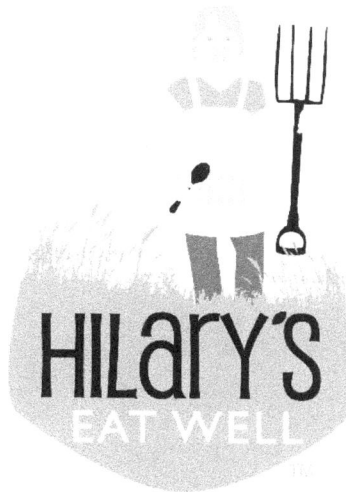

P.O. Box 569
Lawrence, KS 66044
(785) 856 - 3398

hilaryeatswell.com
info@hilaryeatswell.com

Established
2010

Leadership
Hilary Brown, Founder & CEO

Products
Veggie burgers (World's Best, Adzuki Bean, Hemp & Greens, and Root Veggie) and veggie bites

"If you don't feel good, you can't follow your dreams"...

Writing only a 10-page profile on Hilary Brown and her company, Hilary Eats Well, just doesn't work. She's long on personality, strong on outgoingness and she's got a fascinating personal and professional story, which she's more than willing to share.

Alas, under the format of **Small Brand America**, she is limited to her 10-pages, though. So let's not call this a profile, or a chapter, let's call it a preview of a spin-off from this book, **Hilary Eats Well and Gives 'em Hell** (*The Life and Times of Hilary Brown*). Until then, this CliffNotes™ version of her story will have to do.

As a grade-schooler, Hilary was tiny. She was literally like 30 pounds in third grade. She was also unhealthy. She struggled with severe migraines and muscle pain. By junior high, she had tipped the scales the other direction and started to get chubby. Hilary can now reflect back and laugh about the dose of humility you get going through your early teen years as a heavy kid, but it certainly was difficult at the time.

By her senior year of high school, she had found a love for cooking, and she had a real knack for it. For instance, she had the uncanny ability to smell a dish and determine if it needed salt. She enjoyed being around cooking and food so much she elected to skip going to college right out of high school and went to work at a restaurant.

She felt really at home working there but knew staying in the restaurant business would be frowned upon by her family and friends. She felt a need to follow the path her parents had taken and become an educated professional so she headed off to college after sitting on the sidelines for a year.

At college, she studied occupational therapy. After graduation she did become an occupational therapist. The job just never felt right, though. She wanted to do something else; she just wasn't sure what it might be.

While her professional career was floundering, her personal life was suffering as well. She was battling depression, had constant ear infections and continued to suffer from muscle pain.

At the age of 28, Hilary Brown was in a dark hole. She was going through an episode where she was so depressed she couldn't leave the house. She bottomed out one day when she was reduced to a point where she just stared at a wall all day. Feeling life wasn't worth living, she figured out exactly how she would end her life.

As she slept that night, she had a dream where she changed her life and got out of the rut she was in. The warm feeling of pure love engulfed her body.

As she awoke everything was different. Her depression was gone. She finally had some clarity and direction. She began writing, "Do what is in front of you. You don't need to have a plan for your whole life."

While her mental health was better, she was still physically ill. She had gone to doctors with her symptoms but typically wasn't getting any relief, just more prescriptions to take.

This continued until she called yet another doctor to try to get some help. She described her symptoms and got an appointment set. In the meantime, he instructed her to stop eating gluten and dairy.

As she followed the new doctor's orders, she immediately started feeling better. By the time she got into see the doctor, the diagnosis was already complete: Hilary Brown was allergic to the American diet.

As bad as the diagnosis sounds, for Hilary it was like a miracle. For the first time in her life, she finally started feeling good. People started to comment on how much better, and younger, she looked (the consensus was she had lost 10 years). She was free of the headaches and even thinking seemed easier... and she was doing a lot of thinking by the way. She knew it was time to ditch the occupational therapy job.

Hilary had rolled along with a job she didn't really like because she was trying to survive. Now that she was feeling and looking good, she finally felt free to pursue her dreams. "If you don't feel good, you can't follow your dreams," became a personal rally cry for her as she looked to make her career move. Her goal was to put herself into a position where she was going to help others feel good and follow their dreams.

With her affinity for the restaurant business and the knowledge of how her diet change had helped her, Hilary knew her future was in food. She left her job and went to New York to attend the Natural Gourmet Cookery School. Her goal was to learn about natural, organic and gluten-free cooking.

Upon completion of her training in New York, she came back supercharged about locally-sourced ingredients and cooking. She took a paid internship on an urban farm as she worked on a business plan for her own restaurant.

After working on her plan for a few years and getting the courage to do so, she opened a hamburger restaurant called Local Burger. The tagline for the restaurant was, "The World's Most Local Burger." She offered locally sourced grass-fed beef, turkey, elk, bison and veggie burgers.

With all of the great selections on the menu, she was surprised her veggie burger quickly became her second best seller (after the grass-fed beef). Before long, her veggie burger began to transcend the restaurant. Local Burger became known as *the* place to get a veggie burger. They were so popular, she began selling them to other restaurants looking to incorporate a healthy burger alternative on their menu.

In 2010 she began to explore the idea of selling her veggie burgers in grocery stores. It wasn't a business she knew, so she began to meet with various consultants and industry experts. One piece of advice which she took to heart was a consultant who told her, "In the grocery business, people buy on price points."

She took this advice and refined it to make it her own by coming up with the idea of packing her veggie burgers in two-packs. This gave her a great price to offer her product to consumers, and it seemed like a great way to encourage potential customers to give her product a try. Since they may be apprehensive about trying a veggie burger, what better way to appeal to them than to limit their investment and inventory?

In December of 2010 she raised the money she would need to get started in the retail veggie burger business, and Hilary Eats Well was born. Hilary established the following checklist which she viewed as a contract with her customers by setting the standards of what to expect, or not expect (depending on how you look at it), from a Hilary Eats Well product:

- ✓ Healthy fats
- ✓ Gluten free
- ✓ Dairy free
- ✓ Soy free
- ✓ Corn free
- ✓ Yeast free
- ✓ Egg free
- ✓ Nut free

Starting with just a machine called a "Patty-O-Matic®," Hilary Eats Well began pumping out the fully-cooked veggie burgers which only needed to be warmed up in a toaster to serve. They began to make their way to retailers' shelves, but their big break came in the spring of 2012 when introduced into Whole

Foods® stores. Hilary was also successful in securing a deal with United Natural Foods®, Inc., the largest distributor of natural foods in North America.

Hilary is quick to attribute her company's rapid growth to the team she has around her. She notes the talented and intelligent people around her helps Hilary Eats Well accomplish its goals and beyond. She looks forward to introducing more products, allowing people to make smart and delicious eating choices at a price point they can afford.

She marvels at not only the future of her company, but the idea of eating in the future. People finally seem to have had their eyes opened to the pitfalls of eating a diet based on processed foods. She notes that while we are doing a better job of eating local and organic, we haven't even begun to realize the possibilities. Did you know you can eat the entire cattail plant? Well Hilary does. She's wonky that way. Things like that nugget help drive Hilary and keep her curious about the future of healthy eating.

With that, we have reached the end of Hilary's chapter. We haven't even gotten into the movie, the corporate espionage or the erotica yet. It looks like if you want to learn more, you'll just have to wait for the book!

Hilary Eats Well Photo Album

Hilary Brown

Hilary Brown (L/Founder & CEO – R/Cartoon Logo…not bad!)

Inside Hilary Eats Well headquarters

The production line

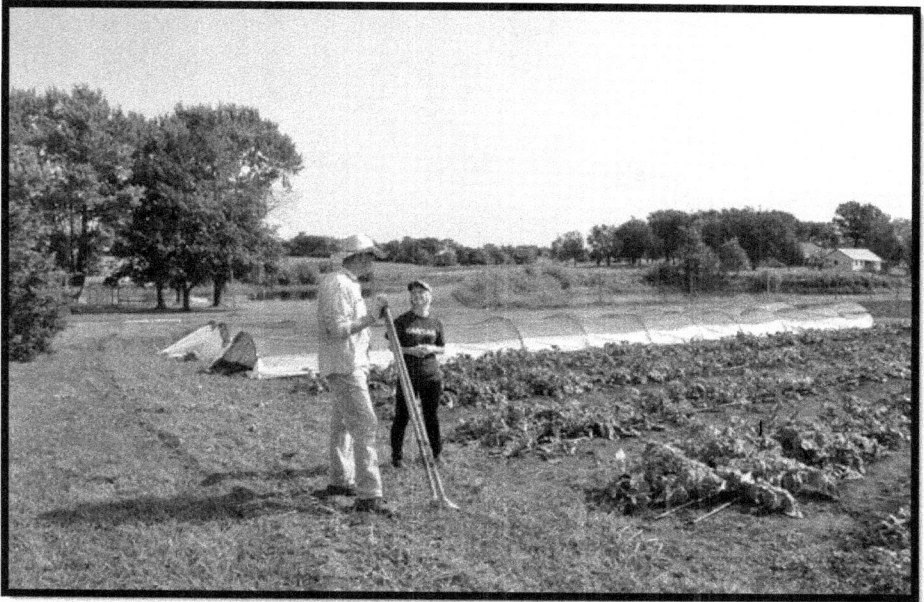

It all starts out in the garden

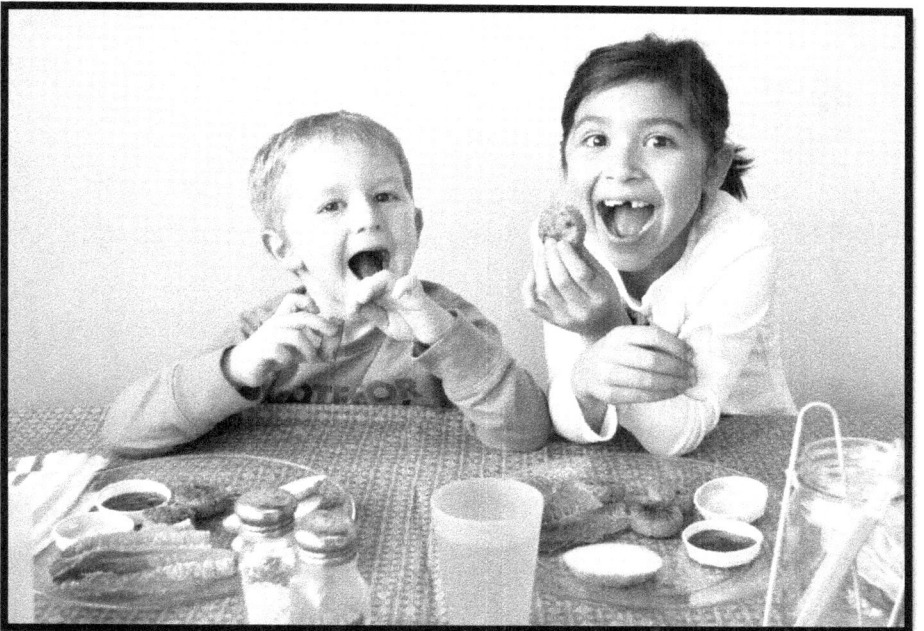

Hilary Eats Well helping kids enjoy their veggies

A look at the World's Best Veggie Burger

Hilary's checklist which serves as the backbone of the company

Hilary Eats Well product lineup

Author's Notes/Resources

The stories of the small companies featured in **Small Brand America** were incredibly fascinating to put together. It seemed like each one was more interesting than the last one as I was interviewing them. My favorite was simply the one I was speaking to at the time since each person was so great in their own way. Whether a small brand had broken through to national distribution, or they were simply fulfilling a need in their hometown, I grew very fond of the individuals who own these companies and their hard work and dedication to the brands they are trying to build.

It's not easy competing on a playing field where you are set-up to fail. The grocery industry caters to, and is fueled by, the large national companies with huge budgets to generate consumer interest and get their items on the shelves. It literally takes millions of dollars to secure shelf space for new product lines for these major companies. Stores automatically want these brands over the smaller competitors because megabrands pay to generate consumer interest via advertising, pay the stores to promote the product and pay to get their product in the stores' warehouses and on their shelves.

As an author, and a consumer, I'm not in any way against the megabrands. For me, though, there is something comforting and even a little fun to think about individuals competing against these giant corporations one consumer at a time.

I do suggest learning more about the companies featured in the book and their products. The more you know about them, and the hard work they are doing to try to get to know you, the more you are likely to try their products. You might just find something you like better than the same brands you've always purchased, simply because "you've always purchased them."

Here's a look at the websites for each:

Aiko Pops – *aikopops.com*
Anarchy in a Jar – *anarchyinajar.com*
Bobby Sue's Nuts - *bobbysuesnuts.com*
Brooklyn Salsa Company - *bksalsa.com*
Casa Visco – *casavisco.com*
Catskill Provisions – *catskillprovisions.com*
Daisy Organic Flour – *daisyflour.com*
Dave's Gourmet, Inc. – *davesgourmet.com*
Denver Bacon Company – *denverbacon.com*
Fatman's Beef Jerky – *fatmansbeefjerky.com*
Great Divide Brewing Co. – *greatdivide.com*
Gus' Pretzels – *guspretzels.com*
Hancock Gourmet Lobster Co. – *hancockgourmetlobster.com*
Hilary Eats Well – *hilaryeatswell.com*
The James Gang BBQ Company – *jamesgangbbq.com*
Jonboy Caramels – *jonboycaramels.com*
Mystic Pizza Company – *mysticpizza.com*
Rockerbox Garlic - *rockerboxgarlic.com*
Sarkisian Specialty Coffee – *sarkisiancoffee.com*
Sun Valley Mustard – *sunvalleymustard.com*
Symple Foods – *symplefoods.com*
Theodent – *theodent.com*
Three Twins Ice Cream – *threetwinsicecream.com*
Tennessee Gourmet – *tngourmetsauce.com*
Upfront Foods – *upfrontfoods.com*

Bibliography/Sources

*In addition to the websites of the companies profiled (all listed in the **Author's Notes/Resources** section), the following resources were also utilized to create this book:*

The Free Dictionary Website: *thefreedictionary.com* (anarchy definition).

Interview with Aiko Pops Owner/"Smooth Poperator" Christopher Mosera: January 7, 2014.

Interview with Anarchy in a Jar Founder & President Laena McCarthy: January 28, 2014.

Interview with Bobby Sue's Nuts CFO Andy Kobren: August 20, 2013.

Interview with Brooklyn Salsa Company Cofounders Rob Behnke and Matt Burns: August 14, 2013.

Interview with Casa Visco VP of Sales & Marketing and Owner Adine Viscusi: January 30, 2014.

Interview with Catskill Provisions, Inc. Co-Founder and Beekeeper Clare Marin: February 10, 2014.

Interview with Daisy Organic Flour President Dave Poorbaugh: December 31, 2013.

Interview with Dave's Gourmet, Inc. President & Founder Dave Hirschkop: February 13, 2014.

Interview with Denver Bacon Company Co-Founder Eric Clayman: February 10, 2014.

Interview with Fatman's Beef Jerky Owner Rick Robey: December 23, 2013.

Interview with Great Divide Brewing Co. Founder/President Brian Dunn: January 9, 2014.

Interview with Gus' Pretzels Owners Gus & Suzanne Koebbe: March 2, 2014.

Interview with Hancock Gourmet Lobster Co. Owner Cal Hancock: February 17, 2014.

Interview with Hilary Eats Well Founder and CEO Hilary Brown: January 13, 2014.

Interview with The James Gang BBQ Company Owner Jesse James: February 11, 2014.

Interview with Jonboy Caramels Co-Owner Jason Alm: February 8, 2014.

Interview with Mystic Pizza General Manager P.J. Pawlis: December 31, 2013.

Interview with Rockerbox Garlic Owner Rae Rotindo: November 6, 2013.

Interview with Sarkisian Specialty Coffee President Debra Sarkisian: February 10, 2014.

Interview with Sun Valley Mustard Owner Joshua R. Wells: January 9, 2014.

Interview with Symple Foods Owner Jean-Pierre Parent: January 27, 2014.

Interview with Theodent Operations and Media Director Jantzen Hubbard: January 16, 2014.

Interview with Three Twins Ice Cream Founder and Owner Neal Gottlieb: January 23, 2014.

Interview with Tennessee Gourmet Owner & President Sue Sykes: November 19, 2013.

Interview with Upfront Foods Founder/President Gigi Twist: January 14, 2014.

Photographs
All photographs, in the sections of each business featured, have been utilized with permission from the respective companies with the following exceptions:

Anarchy in a Jar
Laena McCarthy (Zack DeZon), Laena Cooking (Michael Harlan Turkell), Clementine Rounds (Michael Harlan Turkell), Lemons (Michael Harlan Turkell) & Anarchy Staff (Maureen Post)

Special Thanks

To my mom, Sandy Akley, for her help in editing this book.

Thanks to my wife Amy and to my daughter Cat for just being themselves.

Hats off to Mark Hansen (*mappersmark@gmail.com*) for the great cover design. He's the greatest graphic artist you will ever find!

The following individuals from the featured companies not only couldn't have been nicer, without their help this book would not have been possible:

Jason Alm, Jonboy Caramels

Rob Behnke, The Brooklyn Salsa Company

Hilary Brown, Hilary Eats Well

Matt Burns, The Brooklyn Salsa Company

Doug Christie, Great Divide Brewing Co.

Eric Clayman, Denver Bacon Company

Brian Dunn, Great Divide Brewing Co.

Neal Gottlieb, Three Twins Ice Cream

Cal Hancock, Hancock Gourmet Lobster Co.

Becky Harpstrite, Hilary Eats Well

Dave Hirschkop, Dave's Gourmet, Inc.

Jantzen Hubbard, Theodent

Morgan Imrie, Dave's Gourmet, Inc.

Jesse James, The James Gang BBQ Company

Andy Kobren, Bobby Sue's Nuts

Gus & Suzanne Koebbe, Gus' Pretzels

Claire Marin, Catskill Provisions, Inc.

Laena McCarthy, Anarchy in a Jar

Christopher Mosera, Aiko Pops

Jean-Pierre Parent, Symple Foods

Ashley Pawlis, Mystic Pizza Company

P.J. Pawlis, Mystic Pizza Company

Dave Poorbaugh, Daisy Organic Flour

Marcus Rietema, Three Twins Ice Cream

Rae Rotindo, Rockerbox Garlic

Debra Sarkisian, Sarkisian Specialty Coffee

Sarah Schuerhoff, Three Twins Ice Cream

Sue Sykes, Tennessee Gourmet

Gigi Twist, Upfront Foods, LLC

Adine Viscusi, Casa Visco

Joshua Wells, Sun Valley Mustard

Lastly, lots of love for my father, Larry Akley. He's always with us in spirit.

In Loving Memory of Larry Akley
1942 – 2012

Dad's badge photo compliments of Kelly Brooks (thanks sis!)

Love A Cat Charity – Honolulu, Hawai'i

Steve Akley proudly supports the mission of Love A Cat Charity with a donation from the proceeds of the sale of all of his books.

Mission Statement

Love A Cat Charity's mission is to help end euthanasia of unwanted cats by caring for feral and abandoned felines, spaying or neutering them and, when appropriate, adopting them out. Love A Cat Charity emphasizes the use of Trap-Neuter-Return (TNR) technique to humanely control feral cat populations. Cats are humanely trapped, spayed or neutered and returned to their outdoor homes. TNR improves the cats' health and stabilizes the colony while allowing them to live out their lives outdoors. No new kittens are born and the cats no longer experience the stresses of mating and pregnancy.

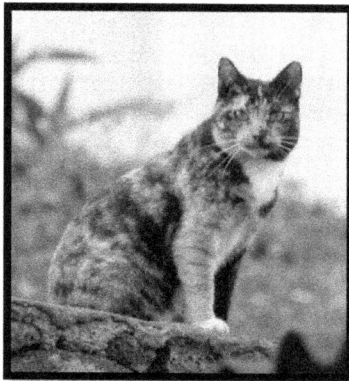

Support of Love A Cat Charity in Honolulu, HI, helps cats like this sweet kitty

Love A Cat Charity
P.O. Box 11753
Honolulu, HI 96828
loveacatcharity.org

About the Author

Steve Akley is a lifelong St. Louis resident. Small Brand America II is his seventh published book. Sign up for his newsletter, or check out his latest work, on his website: steveakley.com. Steve also maintains an author's page on Amazon.com. Just search his name on the site. He can be reached via email: info@steveakley.com.

Find Steve on Social Media

 @steveakley WORDPRESS & Steve Akley

Also by Steve Akley

Be sure to check out Steve's website:

www.steveakley.com

www.ingramcontent.com/pod-product-compliance
Lightning Source LLC
Chambersburg PA
CBHW060544200326
41521CB00007B/480